THE FARMERS' MARKET
family cookbook

THE FARMERS' MARKET
family cookbook

**Recipes from the Murdoch Books
Test Kitchen**

MURDOCH BOOKS

contents

INTRODUCTION

Most shoppers are growing tired of overpriced and flavourless supermarket produce and turning to more traditional food retail outlets — their local farmer's and grower's markets.

*I*n developed countries, the weekly expedition to the supermarket to stock up on necessary supplies has become routine. Everything you need to run a household can be procured there; from detergents to deli items, greeting cards to green vegetables and frozen sweet treats to fresh fruits, meats and fish. Convenient and one-stop, those wide aisles, piercing fluorescent lights and commodious trolleys make food shopping a no-brainer—in fact, we've almost forgotten that there was once an entirely different way to hunt and gather.

Over the past decade, there has been a quiet but significant shift in food shopping options with the rise of grower's and farmer's markets. Ironically, this represents a return to more traditional food retail and a time when every town had its own market. Farmers would typically bring their produce—freshly dug, picked or gathered—and sell direct to buyers. There were no middle-men, no transportation issues, no drawn-out storage, no gas-induced ripening, no specially-developed varieties bred to withstand the rigours of long-distance distribution and supply. In fact, nothing fancy at all—just good, simple, honest food, delivered at its seasonal peak.

While it is a sad fact that many of our seasonal foods have been reduced to mere commodity items (think of tomatoes, apples or strawberries, for example), thankfully not everyone is prepared to settle for the attendant loss of both flavour and varietal quirks that go with it. While it is handy to have salad vegetables in the dead of winter, or out-of-season produce shipped in from far-flung hemispheres, there is no doubt that a rising number of cooks are instead returning to such under-threat values as 'flavour', 'seasonal usage', 'heirloom varieties' and 'boutique-scale production'.

To an extent, this interest is driven by a modern breed of restaurant chef, who increasingly favours 'top quality seasonal produce cooked simply'. Another contributing factor is fatigue with our complex, rat-race lifestyle and a nostalgic yearning for the values of a slower time when one ate what the earth offered up when it saw fit, and each season's bounty was a refreshing change from the previous one. International travel and exposure to true food cultures has done much to alert us to the emptiness of a wholly supermarket-dependent existence.

The fact is, we've become increasingly separated from the source of our food. But grower's markets, and the spirit that motivates them, are bridging this gap. Urbanites can't hope to turn back clocks and exist in rural idylls, but they can, through patronage of a local market, move closer to that place and the person that is the source of their food—and be enriched in the process.

Shopping at grower's markets requires thought, planning and effort but the results are not just superior-flavoured food. Ambling, basket-in-arm, through stalls bursting with fragrantly ripe fruits and just-dug potatoes splotched with rich, damp earth is as much nourishment for the soul as it is for the body. Stall-holders offer tastings, insights, advice and information that often can't be found elsewhere. Buying in-season represents better monetary value, too. Gluts provide the opportunitiy to make jams and preserves, and to freeze such fleeting delights as cherries, apricots and figs for out-of-season use. There's no wasteful packaging or exposure to blinding display lights (which can diminish nutrient content and shorten produce life) at the market, not to mention the refreshing absence of congested check-outs and harried shoppers.

Not everyone, though, has access to a grower's market, and in such instances, sleuthing to find a reputable greengrocer becomes necessary. Find a purveyor who is passionate about their suppliers and produce, who can give you information about fruit and vegetable varieties and details about how, when and where they were grown. Settle for nothing less than perfectly in-season, full-flavoured produce, cook them beautifully and reconnect with the seasonal rhythms that give such a meaningful pace to each and every year.

CHAPTER ONE

vegetables

beetroot • watercress • onions
mushrooms • sweet potatoes • broad beans
artichokes • pumpkins

baby beetroot & tatsoi salad with honey-mustard dressing

serves 4

1.6 kg (3 lb 8 oz/2 bunches) baby
  beetroot (beets)
250 g (9 oz/1⅔ cups) broad (fava)
  beans, shelled
200 g (7 oz/1 bunch) tatsoi

dressing

80 ml (2½ fl oz/⅓ cup) olive oil
1 tablespoon lemon juice
1 tablespoon whole-grain mustard
1 tablespoon honey

Wearing rubber gloves, trim baby beets, discard stalks and reserve unblemished leaves.

Bring a medium saucepan of water to a boil. Add the beets and simmer covered for 8–10 minutes or until tender, then drain. Ease off the skins, pat dry with paper towels, and rinse. Put the beets in a large shallow bowl.

Bring a small saucepan of water to a boil. Add the fava beans and a large pinch of salt and simmer for 2–3 minutes, then drain. When cool enough to handle, slip the beans out of their skins and add to the beets. Add the reserved beet leaves and the small inner leaves of the tatsoi.

To make the dressing, put all of the ingredients in a small bowl and whisk well to combine. Season with salt and freshly ground black pepper to taste. Pour over the beet mixture and toss gently. Serve warm or at room temperature.

Note: Tatsoi is a type of bok choy. In some stores, you may find it referred to as 'rosette bok choy'.

lamb, bean & potato salad with almond garlic sauce

serves 6

800 g (1 lb 12 oz) small boiling potatoes, peeled

600 g (1 lb 5 oz) green beans, trimmed

2 tablespoons olive oil

800 g (1 lb 12 oz) lamb backstraps or loin fillets, trimmed

100 g ($3\frac{1}{2}$ oz/$\frac{1}{2}$ cup) small black olives

120 g ($4\frac{1}{4}$ oz/4 cups) watercress sprigs

90 g ($3\frac{1}{4}$ oz/1 bunch) coriander (cilantro), leaves picked

almond garlic sauce

1 egg yolk

2 tablespoons ground almonds

4 garlic cloves, crushed

$1\frac{1}{2}$ teaspoons dijon mustard

$1\frac{1}{2}$ tablespoons white wine vinegar

60 ml (2 fl oz/$\frac{1}{4}$ cup) walnut oil

Preheat the oven to 200ºC (400ºF/Gas 6). Put the potatoes in a saucepan, cover with water and bring to the boil. Cook for 10 minutes, or until tender. Remove from the saucepan with a slotted spoon and set aside. Add the beans to the boiling water and cook for 4 minutes, or until tender. Remove from the saucepan, refresh under cold running water, then drain well and set aside.

Heat the olive oil in a large, heavy-based ovenproof frying pan until very hot. Season the lamb with sea salt and freshly ground black pepper and sear for 1 minute on eachside, then transfer the pan to the oven and roast the lamb for 8–10 minutes, or until cooked but still pink in the middle. Remove the lamb to a plate and allow to cool to room temperature.

Thinly slice the lamb on the diagonal and place in a large bowl. Slice the cooled potatoes and add to the lamb with the remaining salad ingredients.

To make the almond garlic sauce, put the egg yolk, ground almonds, garlic, mustard and vinegar in a mini food processor, then blend until smooth and well combined. With the motor running, add the walnut oil a teaspoon or so at time, until a smooth, thick sauce forms. Slowly add 2 tablespoons boiling water and blend just until well combined; the sauce should be thick and smooth. Season to taste with sea salt and freshly ground black pepper.

Add enough sauce to the salad to just coat, tossing well. Divide among plates or shallow bowls, drizzle with a little more of the sauce and serve the remaining sauce separately.

salade niçoise

4 waxy potatoes
1 tablespoon olive oil
200 g small green beans, halved
300 g canned tuna in oil, drained
200 g green lettuce leaves
150 g cherry tomatoes, halved
20 black olives, pitted
2 tablespoons capers
3 hard-boiled eggs, cut into
  wedges
8 anchovies

vinaigrette

1 garlic clove, crushed
1 teaspoon Dijon mustard
2 tablespoons white wine vinegar
1 teaspoon lemon juice
125 ml olive oil

Cook the potatoes in boiling salted water for 15 minutes or until just tender. Drain, cut into small cubes and place in a bowl. Drizzle with the olive oil and toss well. Cook the green beans in boiling salted water for 3 minutes, then drain and refresh under cold water. Keep on one side.

To make the vinaigrette, whisk together the garlic, mustard, vinegar and lemon juice. Add the oil in a thin steady stream, whisking until smooth.

Put the tuna in a bowl and separate into large chunks with a fork. Cover the base of a serving dish with the lettuce leaves. Scatter the potatoes, beans, tuna, tomatoes, olives and capers over the leaves, pour the vinaigrette over the top and decorate with the egg and anchovies.

summer salad of mixed salad greens, mango, avocado & shrimp

serves 4

Avocados have soft, buttery flesh, a mild, slightly nutty flavour, and skins that may be smooth or rough. Cut avocado turns brown, so brush it with lemon juice to prevent discoloration. Firm, unripe avocados will ripen at room temperature after 3–4 days.

dressing

⅓ cup olive oil

1 tablespoon white wine vinegar

1 tablespoon dijon mustard

1 teaspoon orange zest, grated

21 ounces raw medium shrimp,
    peeled and deveined, tails intact

1 small red onion

2 avocados

2 mangoes

1 head baby romaine lettuce

½ head red oakleaf lettuce

½ head boston lettuce

To make the dressing, put the olive oil, vinegar, mustard, and orange zest in a small bowl and mix well. Season with salt and freshly ground black pepper to taste.

Preheat a grill or charbroil pan to medium heat. Brush the shrimp with a little of the dressing. Arrange on the grill plate or pan and cook for 5 minutes or until crisp and opaque. Transfer to a large bowl.

Finely slice the onion lengthwise and add to the bowl. Slice the avocados into large wedges and add to the bowl. Slice the mangoes in half and peel them. Cut into slices and add to the bowl.

Discard the damaged outer leaves of the lettuces and tear the leaves into smaller pieces. Add to the bowl. Pour in the dressing and toss lightly before serving.

SELECTION & STORAGE

avocado

Avocados should only be used when fully ripe, otherwise they are hard and completely tasteless. To determine ripeness, cradle the fruit in your hands and apply slight pressure—it should 'give' slightly.

Avocados are perishable so, unless you plan to use them straight away, it is best to purchase them a little under-ripe—they will only take 2–3 days to fully soften at room temperature. Once ripe, store them in the refrigerator and plan on using them within 1–2 days.

broccoli

When buying broccoli, look for heads with tightly closed, compact, deep green florets, with no signs of yellowing. Broccoli with yellow flowers attached is over-mature and should be avoided. The stalks should be firm and not too thick or they will be woody. Any leaves attached to the stalk should be green and sprightly.

A fairly perishable vegetable, broccoli should be stored in a perforated or open plastic bag in the refrigerator crisper and used within 3–4 days. It should not be washed before storing, as water clinging to its surface will cause it to rapidly deteriorate.

Broccolini, which is a recent innovation and an Australian-developed hybrid, should have long, firm, clean stems topped with a smallish, compact head. Florets should be blue-green or green-purple in colour and leaves should be healthy looking (no wilting or browning) and olive green. A few yellow flowers per bunch are acceptable (about six or so) but more than this indicate over-maturity. Store in the same manner as broccoli.

capsicum

Choose capsicums that are heavy for their size and that have bright, tight, smooth, glossy skin with no watery-looking spots or wrinkled patches.

Capsicums are prone to mould and wrinkling, so store them in a ventilated bag in the crisper section of the refrigerator for up to 1 week.

corn

You can tell by the cuts to their stems how long ago corn was harvested—the fresher the cuts, the fresher the corn.

The cobs should feel and look moist and plump, with the kernels inside fat and shiny. Press against the husk and you should be able to feel the kernels within. The silk of the corn should also be a little sticky and look glossy, stiff and moist. Store corn, in its husks, in the refrigerator for 2–3 days only.

spinach (silverbeet)

When buying bunches of spinach, look for those with broad, spade-shaped, jade leaves and undamaged stems. Baby English spinach leaves can also be bought either loose or in pre-packed bags. These are an ideal salad green, but take care to choose small, dry leaves with no bruising, wilting or yellowing as they are extremely perishable.

Spinach needs to be washed carefully in several changes of cold water to eliminate any muddy residue

A delicate green, prone to bruising and other leaf damage, spinach shouldn't be stored for longer than 2 days in a plastic bag in the refrigerator.

zucchini (courgette)

Zucchini represent just one of the many 'summer' or 'tender' squashes available—there is also the crookneck squash; the round globe squash; the oval squash, like the scallopini; or pattypan squash. Pattypan squash are prized for their flesh which, when young and in prime condition, is buttery and dense. These squash are usually a distinctive yellow colour, but can also be either deep bright or pale green.

Choose small firm squash and steam them whole, for about 8–10 minutes, or until tender. Larger ones can be par-boiled for a few minutes, the insides scooped out, replaced with a stuffing and then baked. A fresh breadcrumb stuffing with plenty of chopped fresh herbs (basil, parsley, oregano) and parmesan cheese works beautifully.

tomatoes

The test of a great tomato is in the aroma – sniff the stem and you should be able to detect a strong, sweet-acid smell.

Tomatoes that have been fully ripened on their vines by the sun are terribly perishable, which is why, for supermarket sale, they are picked while green. These tomatoes are then ripened to redness, or sunny yellowness, in controlled environments using ethylene gas and, even though they may look the part, their flavour, aroma and texture never fully develop.

Choose tomatoes that are plump-looking and shiny and that 'give' slightly to pressure when pressed. They should feel heavy for their size and, needless to say, be free of soft spots, blemishes and bruises. Tomatoes with such skin damage will quickly turn mouldy and spoil.

Tomatoes should be stored at cool room temperature, out of their packaging and definitely not in the refrigerator—and used within a few days.

The refrigerator diminishes the flavour of tomatoes; as a sub-tropical fruit, they do not like the cold. If you purchase under-ripe tomatoes (those with green 'shoulders' or the occasional green patch, for example) they will ripen fully, given the right conditions. Leave them somewhere warm and in full sunlight if possible.

The best way to store a glut of tomatoes for future use is by freezing. This can most easily be done by simply freezing them whole—once they thaw the skins will slip easily off and you just need to cut away the stem end. Alternatively, they can be frozen peeled and chopped or peeled and pureed.

fragrant tofu &
tomato soup

serves 4

Paste
½ teaspoon dried shrimp paste

1 teaspoon small dried prawns
(shrimp)

4 Asian shallots, roughly chopped

½ teaspoon white peppercorns

2 coriander (cilantro) roots

1 garlic clove, chopped

2 teaspoons grated ginger

1 tablespoon vegetable oil

750 ml (3 cups) chicken stock or
water

3 tablespoons tamarind purée

1 tablespoon palm sugar

2 tablespoons fish sauce

3 cm (1¼ inch) piece of ginger,
julienned

3 Asian shallots, smashed with the
flat side of a cleaver

300 g (10 oz) silken tofu (bean
curd), cut into 2 cm (¾ inch)
cubes

2 tomatoes, each cut into
8 wedges

1 tablespoon lime juice

2 tablespoons coriander (cilantro)
leaves, for garnish

To make the paste, use a pestle and mortar or food processor to pound or blend the shrimp paste, dried prawns, shallots, peppercorns, coriander roots, garlic and ginger together.

Heat the oil in a saucepan over a low heat, add the paste and cook for 10 to 15 seconds, stirring constantly. Add the stock or water, tamarind purée, palm sugar, fish sauce and ginger. Simmer for 5 minutes to soften the ginger.

Add the shallots, tofu, tomatoes and lime juice to the pan and cook for 2 to 3 minutes to heat through. Garnish with coriander leaves.

ratatouille

serves 4

4 tomatoes
2 tablespoons olive oil
1 large onion, diced
1 red pepper, diced
1 yellow pepper, diced
1 aubergine, diced
2 courgettes, diced

1 teaspoon tomato purée
½ teaspoon sugar
1 bay leaf
3 thyme sprigs
2 basil sprigs
1 garlic clove, crushed
1 tablespoon chopped parsley

Score a cross in the top of each tomato, plunge into boiling water for 20 seconds and then peel the skin away from the cross. Chop roughly.

Heat the oil in a frying pan. Add the onion and cook over low heat for 5 minutes. Add the peppers and cook, stirring, for 4 minutes. Remove from the pan and set aside.

Fry the aubergine until lightly browned all over and then remove from the pan. Fry the courgette until browned and then return the onion, peppers and aubergine to the pan. Add the tomato purée, stir well and cook for 2 minutes. Add the tomato, sugar, bay leaf, thyme and basil, stir well, cover and cook for 15 minutes. Remove the bay leaf, thyme and basil.

Mix together the garlic and parsley and add to the ratatouille at the last minute. Stir and serve.

vegetable tian

serves 6–8 as a side dish

1 kg (2 lb 4 oz) red capsicums
(peppers)

125 ml (4 fl oz/½ cup) olive oil

2 tablespoons pine nuts

800 g (1 lb 10 oz) silverbeet
(Swiss chard), stems removed
and the leaves coarsely
shredded

freshly ground nutmeg, to taste

1 onion, chopped

2 garlic cloves

2 teaspoons chopped thyme

750 g (1 lb 10 oz) tomatoes,
peeled, seeded and diced

1 large eggplant (aubergine),
cut into 1 cm (½ inch) rounds

5 small zucchini (courgettes),
about 500 g (1 lb 2 oz) in total,
thinly sliced on the diagonal

3 ripe tomatoes, cut into 1 cm
(½ inch) slices

1 tablespoon fresh breadcrumbs

4 tablespoons grated parmesan
cheese

30 g (1 oz) unsalted butter,
chopped

Preheat the oven grill (broiler) to high. Cut the capsicums into quarters and remove the seeds and membranes. Grill the capsicums, skin side up, until the skin blackens and blisters. Transfer to a bowl, cover with plastic wrap and leave until cool enough to handle. Slip the blackened skin off the capsicums, then cut the flesh into large strips. Place in a lightly greased 25 x 20 x 5 cm (10 x 8 x 2 inch) baking dish and season lightly with sea salt and freshly ground black pepper.

Preheat the oven to 200°C (400°F/Gas 6). Heat 2 tablespoons of the olive oil in a frying pan. Add the pine nuts and fry over medium heat for 1–2 minutes, or until golden, shaking the pan often so they don't burn. Remove with a slotted spoon and set aside.

Add the silverbeet to the pan and cook for 5 minutes, or until softened. Add the pine nuts and season to taste with sea salt, freshly ground black pepper and nutmeg. Spread the silverbeet mixture over the capsicum slices.

Wipe the pan clean and heat another tablespoon of the olive oil. Add the onion and cook over medium heat for 7–8 minutes, or until soft and golden. Add the garlic and thyme, cook for 1 minute, then add the diced tomato. Bring to the boil, reduce the heat and simmer for 10 minutes. Spread the sauce evenly over the silverbeet.

Wipe the pan clean again and heat the remaining oil. Add the eggplant and cook in batches over high heat for 4–5 minutes on each side, or until golden. Drain on paper towels and place in a single layer over the tomato sauce. Season lightly.

Arrange the zucchini and tomato slices in alternating layers over the eggplant. Sprinkle the breadcrumbs and parmesan over the top, then dot with the butter.

Bake for 25–30 minutes, or until the topping is golden. Serve warm or at room temperature.

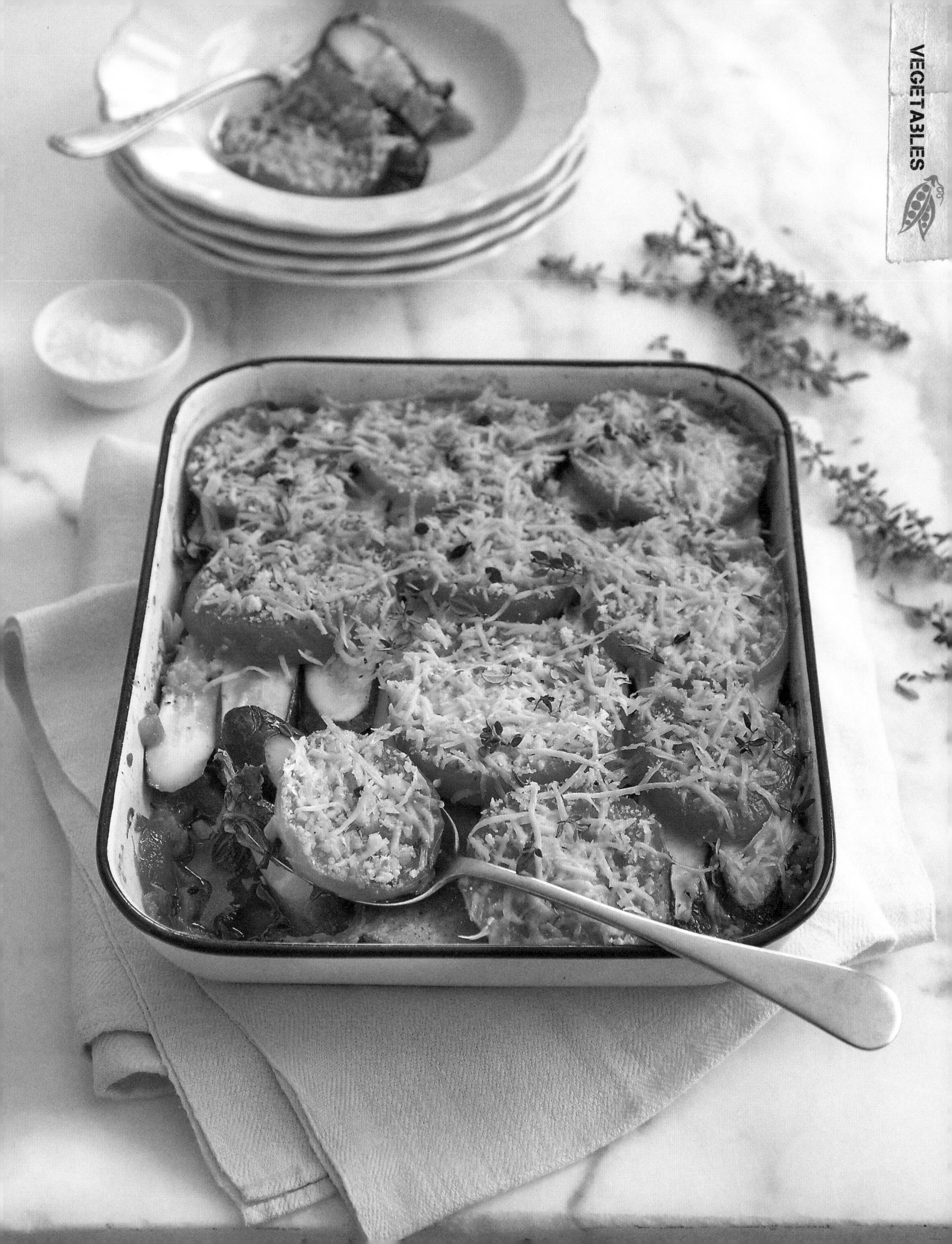

stuffed vegetables provencal

serves 6 as a starter or side dish

2 small eggplants (aubergines), halved lengthways

2 small zucchini (courgettes), halved lengthways

4 tomatoes

2 small red capsicums (peppers)

4 tablespoons olive oil

2 red onions, finely chopped

2 garlic cloves, crushed

250 g (9 oz) minced (ground) pork

250 g (9 oz) minced (ground) veal

3 tablespoons tomato paste (concentrated purée)

4 tablespoons white wine

2 tablespoons chopped parsley

50 g (1¾ oz/½ cup) grated parmesan cheese

80 g (2¾ oz/1 cup) fresh breadcrumbs

extra virgin olive oil, for drizzling

crusty bread, to serve

Preheat the oven to 180°C (350°F/Gas 4). Grease a large roasting tin with olive oil.

Use a spoon to hollow out the centres of the eggplants and zucchini, leaving a border around the edge. Chop the eggplant and zucchini flesh finely and set aside.

Cut the tops off the tomatoes and reserve. Use a spoon to hollow out the centres, catching the juice in a bowl, then chop the flesh roughly. Set the flesh and juice aside. Cut the tops off the capsicums and reserve. Discard the seeds and membranes from inside the capsicum shells. Set the capsicums aside.

Heat half the olive oil in a large frying pan. Add the onion and garlic and sauté over medium–high heat for 3 minutes, or until softened. Add the pork and veal and stir for 5 minutes, or until the meat browns, breaking up any lumps with the back of a fork.

Stir in the chopped eggplant and zucchini flesh and cook for 3 minutes, then stir in the chopped tomato and reserved juice, along with the tomato paste and wine. Cook, stirring occasionally, for 10 minutes. Remove from the heat and stir in the parsley, parmesan and breadcrumbs. Season well with sea salt and freshly ground black pepper, then spoon the mixture into the eggplant, zucchini, tomato and capsicum cavities. Put the tops back on the tomatoes and capsicums.

Arrange the capsicums and eggplant in a single layer in the roasting tin. Drizzle with some of the remaining olive oil, pour 125 ml (4 fl oz/½ cup) water into the roasting tin and bake for 15 minutes. Add the tomatoes to the roasting tin in a single layer and bake for 5 minutes. Finally, add the zucchini in a single layer, drizzle with the remaining olive oil and bake for a further 25 minutes, or until all the vegetables are tender.

Serve hot or at room temperature, drizzled with some extra virgin olive oil, with slices of crusty bread.

corn & polenta pancakes with bacon and maple syrup

serves 4

90 g (3¼ oz/¾ cup) self-raising
  flour
110 g (3¾ oz/¾ cup) fine polenta
310 g (11 oz/1½ cups) sweet corn
  kernels (about 3 cobs)
375 ml (13 fl oz/1½ cups) milk

olive oil, for pan-frying
8 slices of rindless bacon
175 g (6 oz/½ cup) maple syrup or
  golden syrup

Preheat the oven to 120°C (235°F/Gas ½). Sift the flour into a bowl and stir in the polenta. Add the corn and 250 ml (9 fl oz/½ cup) of the milk and stir until just combined. Season with sea salt and freshly ground black pepper, then stir in the remaining milk.

Heat 3 tablespoons olive oil in a large frying pan. Spoon half the batter into the pan to make four 9 cm (3½ inch) pancakes. Cook over medium heat for 2 minutes on each side, or until golden and cooked through. Drain on paper towels and place in the oven to keep warm while cooking the remaining four pancakes, adding more oil if necessary. Transfer to the oven to keep warm.

Add the bacon to the same pan and cook for 5 minutes. Put two pancakes and two bacon slices on each plate and serve drizzled with maple syrup.

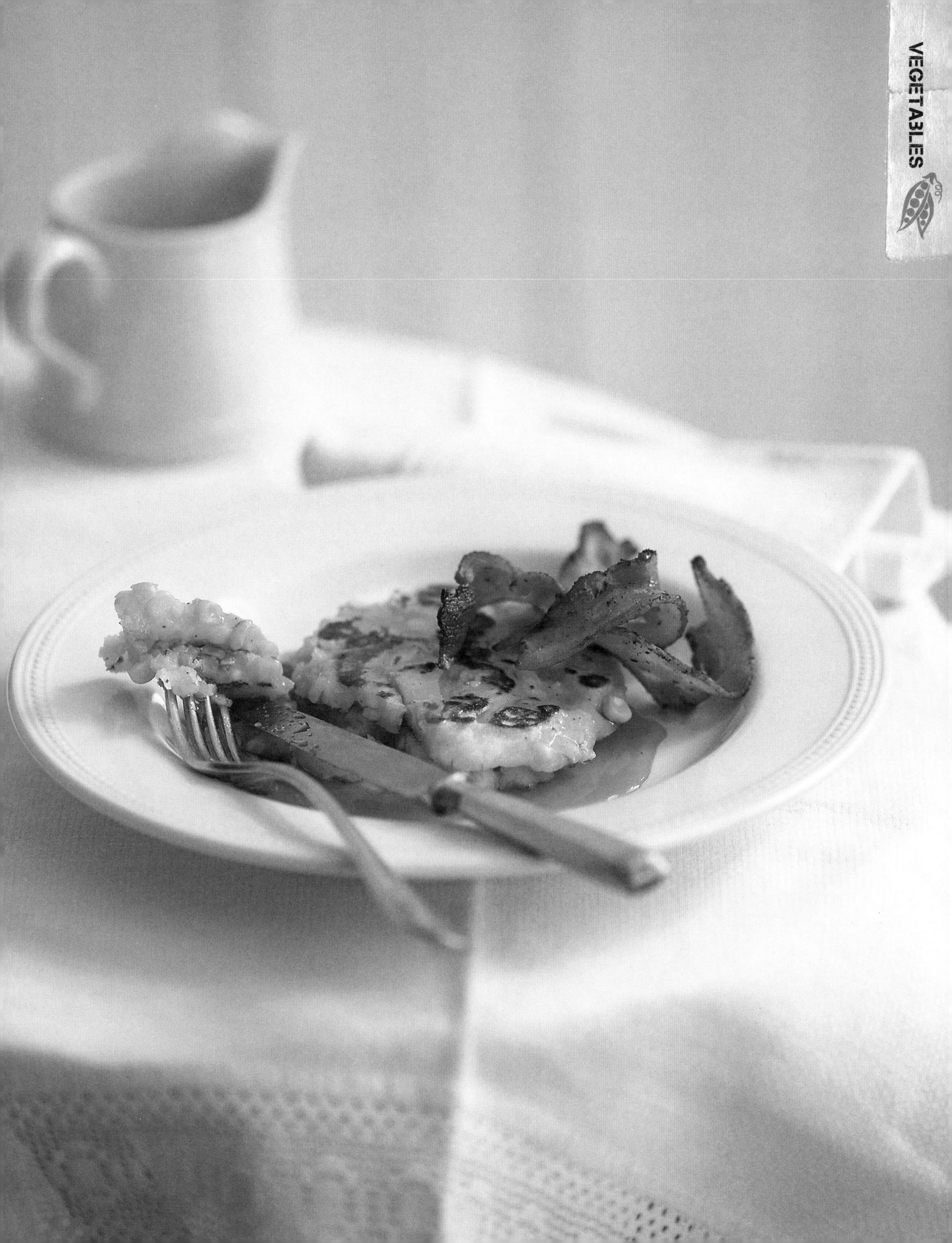

french shallot tatin

serves 6

750 g (1 lb 10 oz) large brown
    shallots, unpeeled

50 g (1¾ oz) unsalted butter,
    plus extra, for greasing

2 tablespoons olive oil

4 tablespoons soft brown sugar

3 tablespoons balsamic vinegar

pastry

125 g (4½ oz/1 cup) plain
    (all-purpose) flour

60 g (2¼ oz) cold unsalted
    butter, chopped

2 teaspoons wholegrain mustard

1 egg yolk, mixed with
    1 tablespoon iced water

Put the shallots in a saucepan of boiling water for 5 minutes to make them easier to peel. Drain well, allow to cool slightly, then peel the shallots, taking care to leave the root ends intact.

Heat the butter and olive oil in a large heavy-based frying pan. Add the shallots and cook over low heat, stirring often, for 15 minutes, or until the shallots have started to soften. Add the sugar, vinegar and 3 tablespoons water and stir to dissolve the sugar. Simmer over low heat for a further 15–20 minutes, or until the liquid has reduced and has become syrupy, turning the shallots occasionally.

To make the pastry, sift the flour and a pinch of sea salt into a large bowl. Using your fingertips, lightly rub the butter and mustard into the flour until the mixture resembles coarse breadcrumbs. Make a well in the centre. Add the egg yolk mixture to the well and mix using a flat-bladed knife until a dough forms. Gently gather the dough together, transfer to a lightly floured surface, then press into a round disc. Cover with plastic wrap and refrigerate for 30 minutes, or until firm.

Meanwhile, preheat the oven to 200°C (400°F/Gas 6).

Grease a shallow 20 cm (8 inch) round sandwich tin with butter. Pack the shallots tightly into the tin and drizzle with any syrup remaining in the frying pan.

On a sheet of baking paper, roll out the pastry to a circle 1 cm (½ inch) larger than the sandwich tin. Lift the pastry into the tin and lightly push it down so it is slightly moulded over the shallots. Bake for 20–25 minutes, or until the pastry is golden brown.

Remove the tart from the oven and allow to stand in the tin on a wire rack for 5 minutes. To serve, place a plate over the tin and carefully turn the tart out, then gently invert the tart onto a serving plate. Serve warm.

Note Shallot tatin is best eaten the day it is made.

zucchini patties

serves 4 as a starter or side dish

cucumber and yoghurt salad

1 Lebanese (short) cucumber

sea salt, for sprinkling

250 g (9 oz/1 cup) Greek-style
  yoghurt

1 small garlic clove, crushed

1 tablespoon chopped dill

2 teaspoons white wine vinegar

ground white pepper, to taste

300 g (10 oz) zucchini
  (courgettes), grated

1 small onion, finely chopped

3 tablespoons self-raising flour

4 tablespoons grated kefalotyri
  or parmesan cheese

1 tablespoon chopped mint

2 teaspoons chopped flat-leaf
  (Italian) parsley

a pinch of ground nutmeg

3 tablespoons dry breadcrumbs

1 egg, lightly beaten

olive oil, for pan-frying

rocket (arugula) leaves, to serve

lemon wedges, to serve (optional)

To make the cucumber and yoghurt salad, chop the cucumber into small pieces, place in a colander, sprinkle with sea salt and set aside in the sink or on a plate to drain for 15–20 minutes.

In a bowl, mix together the yoghurt, garlic, dill and vinegar. Add the cucumber and season to taste with sea salt and ground white pepper. Cover and refrigerate until required.

Meanwhile, preheat the oven to 120ºC (235ºF/Gas ½).Put the zucchini and onion in a clean tea towel (dish towel), gather the corners together and twist as tightly as possible to remove all the juices. Tip the zucchini and onion into a large bowl, then add the flour, cheese, mint, parsley, nutmeg, breadcrumbs and egg. Season well with sea salt and freshly cracked black pepper, then mix with your hands to a stiff batter.

Heat 1 cm (½ inch) olive oil in a large heavy-based frying pan over medium heat. When the oil is hot, drop 2 tablespoons of the batter into the pan and press flat to make a thick patty. Fry several at a time for 2–3 minutes, or until well browned all over. Drain well on paper towels and place in the oven to keep warm while cooking the remaining patties.

Serve hot with rocket leaves, the cucumber and yoghurt salad and lemon wedges, if desired.

broccoli & ricotta souffle

serves 4

60 g (2¼ oz/1 cup) small broccoli
   florets
2 tablespoons olive oil
40 g (1½ oz) unsalted butter
1 onion, finely chopped
1 garlic clove, crushed
400 g (14 oz/scant 1⅔ cups)
   ricotta cheese

50 g (1¾ oz/½ cup) grated
   parmesan cheese
5 egg yolks, lightly beaten
a pinch of nutmeg
a pinch of cayenne pepper
5 egg whites
a pinch of cream of tartar
3 tablespoons dry breadcrumbs

Preheat the oven to 190ºC (375ºF/Gas 5).

Cook the broccoli florets in boiling salted water for 4 minutes, then drain well and roughly chop.

Heat the olive oil and butter in a frying pan. Add the onion and garlic and sauté over medium heat for 5 minutes, or until the onion has softened. Transfer to a large bowl and add the broccoli, ricotta, parmesan, egg yolks, nutmeg and cayenne pepper. Season with sea salt and freshly ground black pepper. Mix well.

In a clean, dry bowl, whisk the egg whites with the cream of tartar and a pinch of sea salt until stiff peaks form. Stir one-third of the beaten egg white into the broccoli mixture to loosen, then gently fold in the remaining egg white.

Grease a 1 litre (35 fl oz/4 cup) soufflé dish. Sprinkle with the breadcrumbs, turn the dish to coat, then shake out the excess. Spoon the broccoli mixture into the dish and bake for 35–40 minutes, or until puffed and golden brown. Serve immediately.

Note: Because this soufflé has a ricotta cheese base, it won't rise as much as a conventional soufflé.

pizza spinaci

makes *two* 30 cm (12 inch) pizzas

1 tablespoon caster
   (superfine) sugar

2 teaspoons active dried yeast,
   or 15 g (½ oz) fresh yeast

210 ml (7½ fl oz) lukewarm water

450 g (1 lb/3⅔ cups) plain
   (all-purpose) flour

¼ teaspoon sea salt

3 tablespoons olive oil

cornflour (cornstarch),
   for dusting

topping

4 tablespoons olive oil, plus
   extra, for brushing

4 garlic cloves, crushed

4 tablespoons pine nuts

1 kg (2 lb 4 oz) baby English
   spinach leaves

400 ml (14 fl oz) ready-made
   tomato pasta sauce

440 g (15½ oz/3 cups) grated
   mozzarella cheese

30 very small black olives

50 g (1¾ oz/½ cup) grated
   parmesan cheese

Put the sugar and yeast in a bowl and stir in 90 ml (3 fl oz) of the lukewarm water. Leave to stand in a draught-free place for 10 minutes, or until foamy.

Mix the flour and sea salt in a large bowl and make a well in the centre. Add the olive oil, remaining lukewarm water and the yeast mixture to the well and mix using a wooden spoon until a rough dough forms. Transfer to a lightly floured surface and knead for 8 minutes, adding a little flour or extra warm water as necessary, until the dough is soft, smooth and elastic.

Place the dough in a large oiled bowl, turning to coat in the oil. Cover with plastic wrap and leave in a draught-free place for 1–1½ hours, or until doubled in size.

Preheat the oven to 240ºC (475ºF/Gas 8) and lightly oil two 30 cm (12 inch) rectangular or round baking trays.

To make the topping, heat the olive oil in a large saucepan, then add the garlic and pine nuts and fry over low heat, stirring often, for 5–6 minutes, or until golden. Add the spinach (in batches if necessary), increase the heat and stir until wilted. Season with sea salt and freshly ground black pepper and set aside.

Gently deflate the dough using a lightly floured fist, then divide in half. Roll out each portion to fit the baking trays. Dust each pizza base with cornflour and spoon half the tomato sauce onto each base, spreading nearly to the edges. Sprinkle with half the mozzarella. Spread the spinach mixture and olives over the top, then sprinkle with the remaining mozzarella and parmesan.

Bake for 12–15 minutes, or until the crust is golden and puffed. Brush the rim with extra olive oil before serving.

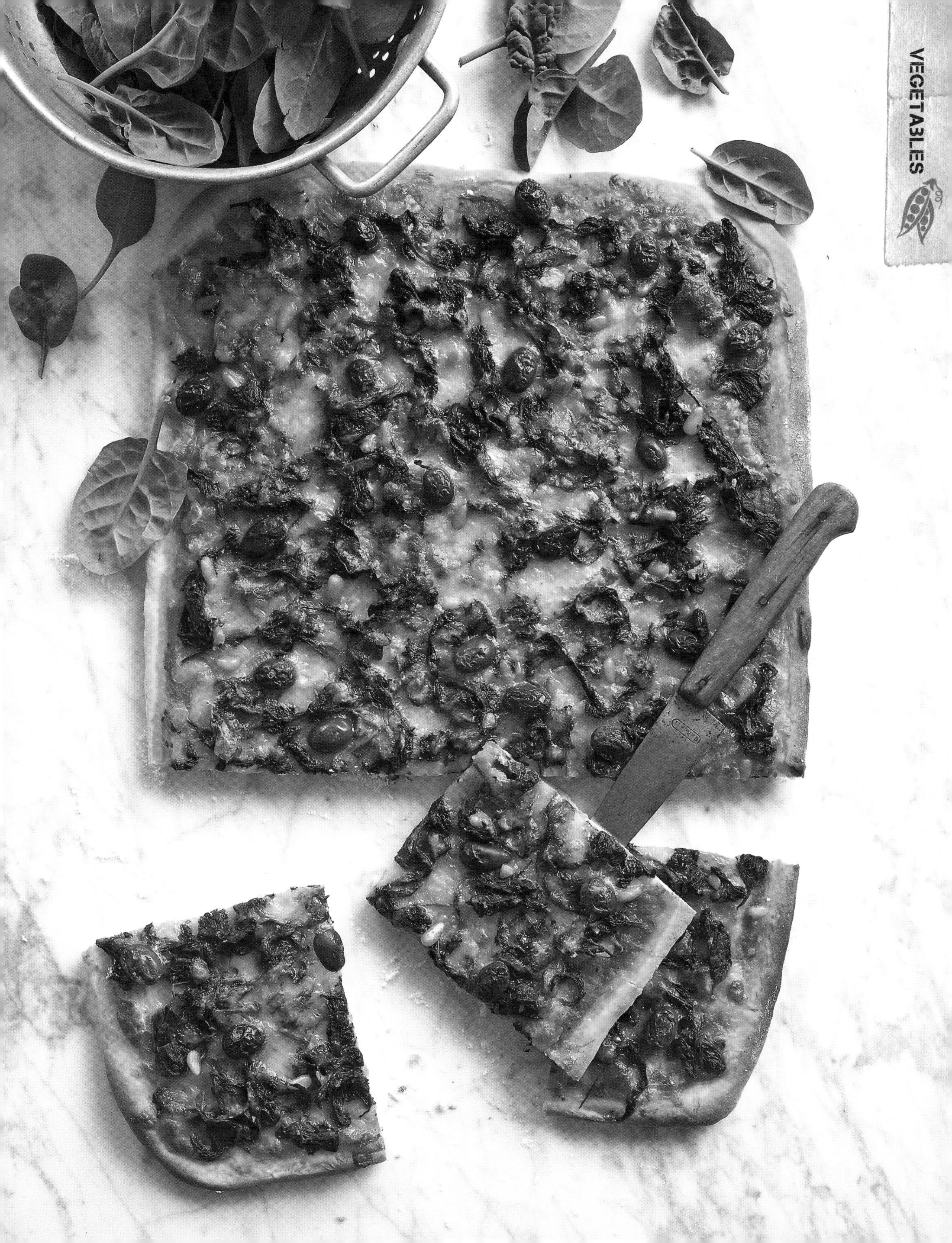

beetroot with skordalia

serves 6 as a starter or side dish

1 kg (2 lb 4 oz) beetroot (beets),
    with leaves attached
3 tablespoons extra virgin olive oil
1 tablespoon red wine vinegar

skordalia
250 g (9 oz) roasting potatoes,
    such as russet (idaho) or king
    edward, peeled and cut into
    2 cm (¾ inch) cubes
2–3 garlic cloves, crushed
½ teaspoon sea salt
ground white pepper, to taste
90 ml (3 fl oz) olive oil
1 tablespoon white vinegar

Cut the stems from the beetroot, leaving 2–3 cm (¾–1¼ inches) attached. Wash the leaves, discarding any tough outer ones. Cut the stems and leaves into 7 cm (2¾ inch) lengths and wash well. Scrub the beetroot bulbs clean.

Bring a large saucepan of salted water to the boil. Add the beetroot bulbs and gently boil for 30–45 minutes, or until tender when pierced with a skewer. Remove with a slotted spoon and cool slightly.

Meanwhile, make the skordalia. Bring another large saucepan of water to the boil, add the potato and cook for 10 minutes, or until very soft. Drain thoroughly, then mash using a masher or potato ricer until quite smooth. Stir in the garlic, sea salt and a pinch of white pepper, then gradually add the olive oil, stirring well with a wooden spoon. Stir in the vinegar and season to taste.

Bring the beetroot water back to the boil. Add leaves (and a little more water if necessary) and boil for 8 minutes, or until tender. Drain well, allow to cool slightly, then squeeze out any excess water from the leaves.

Peel the beetroot, then cut into quarters or thick wedges. Arrange on a serving plate with the leaves. Mix together the extra virgin olive oil and vinegar, season to taste and drizzle over the leaves and bulbs. Serve warm or at room temperature, with the skordalia.

mushroom quiche with parsley pastry

serves 4-6

155 g (5½ oz/1¼ cups) plain (all-purpose) flour

3 tablespoons very finely chopped parsley

90 g (3¼ oz) cold unsalted butter, chopped

1 egg yolk, mixed with 2 tablespoons iced water

mushroom filling

30 g (1 oz) unsalted butter

1 red onion, finely chopped

175 g (6 oz) button mushrooms, sliced

1 teaspoon lemon juice

4 tablespoons chopped parsley

3 tablespoons snipped chives

2 eggs, lightly beaten

170 ml (5½ fl oz/⅔ cup) pouring (whipping) cream

Sift the flour and a pinch of sea salt into a large bowl. Mix the parsley through. Using your fingertips, lightly rub the butter into the flour until the mixture resembles coarse breadcrumbs. Make a well in the centre. Add the egg yolk mixture to the well and mix using a flat-bladed knife until a rough dough forms, adding a little extra iced water if needed. Turn out onto a lightly floured surface and gather into a ball. Cover with plastic wrap and refrigerate for at least 30 minutes.

Roll out the pastry on a sheet of baking paper until large enough to fit the base and side of a 35 x 10 cm (14 x 4 inch) loose-based tart tin. Ease the pastry into the tin and trim the edges. Refrigerate the pastry-lined tin for a further 20 minutes.

Meanwhile, preheat the oven to 190°C (375°F/Gas 5).

Line the pastry shell with baking paper and spread with a layer of baking beads, dried beans or rice.

Bake the pastry for 15 minutes, then remove the paper and baking beads and bake for a further 10 minutes, or until the pastry is dry. Reduce the oven temperature to 180°C (350°F/Gas 4).

To make the mushroom filling, melt the butter in a frying pan, add the onion and sauté over medium heat for 5 minutes, or until softened. Add the mushrooms and sauté for 2–3 minutes, or until soft. Stir in the lemon juice and herbs. Meanwhile, mix the eggs and cream together and season with sea salt and freshly ground black pepper.

Spread the mushroom mixture into the pastry shell and pour the egg mixture over. Bake for 25–30 minutes, or until the filling has set. Serve warm or at room temperature.

Note Mushroom quiche is best served the day it is made.

asparagus & mint frittata

serves 4

6 eggs

35 g (1¼ oz/⅓ cup) grated pecorino or parmesan cheese

1 handful mint leaves, finely shredded

200 g (7 oz or about 16) baby asparagus spears

2 tablespoons extra virgin olive oil

Break the eggs into a large bowl, beat well, then stir in the cheese and mint and set aside. Trim the woody part of the asparagus, then cut on the diagonal into 5 cm (2 inch) pieces.

Heat the oil in a frying pan that has a heatproof handle. Add the asparagus and cook for 5 minutes, or until the asparagus is tender. Season, then reduce the heat to low. Pour the egg mixture over the asparagus and cook for 8–10 minutes. Use a spatula to pull the side of the frittata away from the side of the pan and tip the pan slightly so the uncooked egg runs underneath the frittata.

When the mixture is nearly set but still slightly runny on top, place the pan under a low grill (broiler) for 1–2 minutes, until the top is set. Serve warm or at room temperature.

asparagus

Inspect the stem end and reject any asparagus that is wrinkled, dried out or split. Tips should be tight, bright and clean—pass over ones that look weepy or floppy. Choose spears roughly the same size so they will cook at the same time.

Debate rages over the pros and cons of fat spears versus thin spears, with some claiming one to be vastly superior to the other—but this is not necessarily the case. Buy the freshest asparagus possible and you can't go too wrong with either.

Store asparagus for no longer than 2 days in a plastic bag in the refrigerator.

artichoke

Globe artichokes are in peak condition when their leaves are green and tight and they feel heavy for their size.

The best test for freshness is to rub the leaves together to check for a characteristic 'squeak'. This is often considered a more reliable indicator than colour alone, as artichokes with some bronzing on the tips of their leaves (called the 'winter kiss' in some countries) have been touched by frost, which actually enhances their flavour and makes them the most highly prized of all.

Artichokes are dry and well past their prime when their leaves appear to be opening. They start deteriorating from the moment they are picked so freshness is of the essence. While best used on the day of purchase, unwashed artichokes can be stored in a sealed plastic bag in the refrigerator for up to 2 days.

carrot

Today, carrots are bred for consistency of colour and size. Gone, it seems, are the days of wiggly, misshapen carrots—they all seem to be uniformly straight and thick. Choose mature carrots with smooth, unblemished skin, exhibiting no soft, shrivelled, brown or wrinkled spots. The deeper the orange colour, the higher the betacarotene.levels.

Avoid any with green 'shoulders' as these have been exposed to sunlight and will be bitter. Don't buy overly-large carrots either as these will have a tough, woody core and not taste as sweet.

Generally, carrots are marketed without their luxurious, green tops—if you do happen to buy some with tops on, which should be green and fresh-looking with no signs of wilting or yellowing, cut these off for storage as they will drain the carrots of nutrients and moisture. Greens from extremely fresh young carrots have a distinctive, spicy taste and can be eaten chopped and tossed into a salad or soup.

mushrooms

When buying mushrooms, look for unblemished specimens, with no signs of bruising, tearing or soft spots. The stems should still be intact and the caps firm, not shrivelled, dry or 'tacky', which indicates spoilage.

Store mushrooms in a paper bag (this prevents dehydration and allows them to 'breathe') in the refrigerator for up to 3 days. Mushrooms absorb other flavours, so it is best not to store them near strong-smelling foods.

Mushrooms are porous and readily absorb water—they should not be washed before storing or using. Rather, trim stems, then lightly dust with a pastry brush or carefully wipe with a damp cloth to remove any dirt clinging to their surface. As with all rules, there is of course an exception—morels need to be thoroughly washed as bugs can hide in their hollow centres.

If planning to cook mushrooms whole then choose uniform-sized specimens so that they cook in approximately the same amount of time.

pumpkin (winter squash)

Whole pumpkins are very good keepers if stored in the right conditions. They should be unblemished and have thick skin, with an amount of stalk remaining to protect the interior from damp.

Buy what is locally grown and seasonally available, according to your needs. For example, a hubbard can weigh over 5 kg (11 lb) and once cut needs to be used within a few days or it will quickly become mouldy—so decide how much you can deal with at a time before you buy. Butternut pumpkins or the so-called jap and kent pumpkins are a more manageable size if leftovers are an issue.

If placed in a cool, well-ventilated place, they will last for several months. Cut pumpkin, as previously noted, is very perishable and should be refrigerated then eaten within a few days. If purchasing cut pieces of pumpkin, select those with bright, gleaming flesh and healthy-looking, moist interiors.

sweet potato

Most sweet potatoes are aged for some weeks in order for their sugars to develop—freshly harvested sweet potatoes are generally not sweet. Choose ones with smooth, unblemished skins, exhibiting no bruises, mould or soft spots.

Only buy as many sweet potatoes as you need because they don't last very long; store them at room temperature in a well-ventilated spot for 2–3 days and not in the refrigerator.

sweet potato ravioli

serves 4

500 g (1 lb 2 oz) orange sweet
   potato, peeled and cut into 2 cm
   ($^3/_4$ inch) chunks

3 tablespoons olive oil

150 g (5$^1/_2$ oz/$^2/_3$ cup) ricotta
   cheese

2 tablespoons grated parmesan
   cheese

1 tablespoon chopped basil

3 garlic cloves, crushed

500 g (1 lb 2 oz) egg won ton
   wrappers

60 g (2$^1/_4$ oz) unsalted butter

310 ml (10$^3/_4$ fl oz/1$^1/_4$ cups)
   pouring (whipping) cream

small basil leaves, to garnish

Preheat the oven to 220ºC (425ºF/Gas 7). Place the sweet potato on a baking tray and drizzle with the olive oil. Bake for 40–45 minutes, or until tender.

Transfer the sweet potato to a bowl. Add the ricotta, parmesan, basil and one-third of the garlic and mash until smooth. Season to taste with sea salt and freshly ground black pepper.

Line a baking tray with baking paper. Cover the won ton wrappers with a damp tea towel (dish towel) to stop them drying out. Place 2 level teaspoons of the sweet potato mixture into the centre of one won ton wrapper and brush the edges with a little water. Top with another wrapper, pressing the edges together to seal. Place on the baking tray and cover with a tea towel. Repeat with the remaining ingredients to make 24 ravioli, placing a sheet of baking paper between each layer on the tray.

Melt the butter in a frying pan. Add the remaining garlic and sauté over medium heat for 1 minute. Add the cream, bring to the boil, then reduce the heat and simmer for 4–5 minutes, or until the cream has reduced and thickened. Cover and keep warm.

Bring a large saucepan of water to the boil. Cook the ravioli in batches for 2–4 minutes, or until just tender. Drain well and divide among warmed serving bowls. Ladle the hot sauce over the top, scatter with basil leaves and serve.

chicken, artichoke & broad bean stew

serves 4

60 g (2¼ oz/½ cup) plain (all-purpose) flour

8 chicken thighs on the bone, skin on

2 tablespoons olive oil

1 large red onion, cut into small wedges

125 ml (4 fl oz/½ cup) dry white wine

250 ml (9 fl oz/1 cup) chicken stock

2 teaspoons finely chopped rosemary

340 g (12 oz) jar of marinated artichoke hearts, drained well and cut into quarters

155 g (5½ oz/1 cup) frozen broad (fava) beans, peeled

potato mash

800 g (1 lb 12 oz) potatoes, peeled and cut into large chunks

60 g (2¼ oz) butter

3 tablespoons chicken stock

Season the flour with sea salt and freshly ground black pepper. Dust the chicken thighs in the flour, shaking off the excess.

Heat the olive oil in a saucepan or flameproof casserole dish. Add the chicken in batches and brown over medium heat for 8 minutes, turning once. Remove and drain on paper towels.

Add the onion to the pan and sauté for 3–4 minutes, or until softened but not browned.

Increase the heat to high, add the wine and boil for 2 minutes, or until reduced to a syrupy consistency. Stir in the stock and bring the mixture just to the boil.

Return the chicken to the pan and add the rosemary. Reduce the heat to low, then cover and simmer for 45 minutes.

Add the artichoke, increase the heat to high and return to the boil. Reduce to a simmer and cook, uncovered, for 10–15 minutes. Add the broad beans and cook for a further 5 minutes.

Meanwhile, make the potato mash. Cook the potato in a saucepan of boiling salted water for 15–20 minutes, or until tender. Drain, then return to the saucepan.

Add the butter and stock and mash well using a potato masher. Spoon the mashed potato into four warmed shallow bowls, then spoon the stew over or around and serve.

lamb & artichoke fricassée

serves 8

6 artichokes
60 ml (2 fl oz/¼ cup) lemon juice
2 large tomatoes
80 ml (2½ fl oz/⅓ cup) olive oil
2 kg (4 lb 8 oz) diced lamb
750 g (1 lb 10 oz) brown onions, thinly sliced
1 tablespoon plain (all-purpose) flour

2 garlic cloves, crushed
185 ml (6 fl oz/¾ cup) white wine
350 ml (12 fl oz/1⅓ cups) ready-made chicken stock
1 bouquet garni
chopped fresh flat-leaf (Italian) parsley, to garnish
lemon wedges, to serve

To prepare the artichokes, bring a large saucepan of salted water to the boil and add the lemon juice. Trim the stems from the artichokes and remove the tough outer leaves. Cut the hard tips off the remaining leaves using scissors. Cook the artichokes for 5 minutes. Remove and turn upside down to drain. When cool enough to handle, use a small spoon to remove the choke from the centre of each. Scrape the bases well to remove all the membrane. Cut the artichokes into quarters and set aside.

Score a cross in the top of each tomato, plunge into boiling water for 20 seconds, transfer to a bowl of iced water to cool, and then peel the skin and discard. Cut each tomato in half and scoop out the seeds with a teaspoon. Chop the tomatoes.

Heat half the oil in a deep heatproof casserole dish and fry batches of the lamb until golden. Add the remaining oil and cook the onion for about 8 minutes, or until soft and caramelized. Add the flour and cook for 1 minute. Add the garlic, tomato, wine and chicken stock. Return the lamb to the pan, add the bouquet garni and simmer, covered, for 1 hour.

Put the artichokes in the casserole dish and simmer, uncovered, for a further 15 minutes. Remove the lamb and artichokes with a slotted spoon and place in a serving dish. Keep warm. Discard the bouquet garni. Cook the sauce over high heat until it thickens. Pour the sauce over the lamb and garnish with parsley. Serve with lemon wedges.

spaghetti with rocket & chilli

serves 4-6

500 g (1 lb 2 oz) spaghetti or
  spaghettini
2 tablespoons olive oil
2 teaspoons finely chopped small
  red chilli

450 g (1 lb) rocket (arugula) leaves
1 tablespoon lemon juice
shaved parmesan cheese, to serve

Cook the pasta in a large saucepan of rapidly boiling salted water until *al dente*. Drain and return to the pan.

Meanwhile, heat the olive oil in a large frying pan. Add the chilli and cook for 1 minute over low heat. Add the rocket and cook, stirring often, for a further 2–3 minutes, or until softened. Add the lemon juice and season with sea salt and freshly ground black pepper.

Add the rocket mixture to the pasta and toss to combine well. Serve scattered with shaved parmesan.

leeks à la grecque

serves 4 as a side dish or starter

3 tablespoons extra virgin olive oil

1½ tablespoons white wine

1 tablespoon tomato paste
    (concentrated purée)

¼ teaspoon sugar

1 bay leaf

1 thyme sprig

1 garlic clove, crushed

4 coriander seeds, crushed

4 peppercorns

8 small leeks, white part only,
    rinsed well

1 teaspoon lemon juice

1 tablespoon chopped parsley

lemon halves or wedges, to serve

Put the olive oil, wine, tomato paste, sugar, bay leaf, thyme, garlic, coriander seeds, peppercorns and 250 ml (9 fl oz/1 cup) water in a large heavy-based frying pan with a lid. Bring to the boil, cover and simmer for 5 minutes.

Add the leeks in a single layer and bring to simmering point. Reduce the heat, then cover and simmer gently for 20–30 minutes, or until the leeks are tender when pierced with a skewer. Drain the leeks well, reserving the liquid, then transfer to a serving dish.

Add the lemon juice to the reserved cooking liquid and boil rapidly for 1 minute, or until the liquid has reduced and is slightly syrupy. Season to taste with sea salt, then strain the sauce over the leeks. Allow to cool, then serve the leeks at room temperature, sprinkled with chopped parsley and with some lemon for squeezing over.

carrot & pumpkin risotto

serves 6

90 g (3¼ oz) unsalted butter
1 onion, finely chopped
400 g (14 oz) pumpkin (winter squash), peeled, seeded and finely chopped to give 300 g (10½ oz/2 cups)
3 carrots, chopped

2 litres (70 fl oz/8 cups) vegetable or chicken stock, approximately
440 g (15½ oz/2 cups) risotto rice
90 g (3¼ oz/1 cup) shaved pecorino or parmesan cheese
¼ teaspoon freshly grated nutmeg
½ teaspoon thyme leaves

Heat 60 g (2¼ oz) of the butter in a large heavy-based saucepan. Add the onion and sauté over medium heat for 2–3 minutes, or until beginning to soften. Add the pumpkin and carrot and cook for 6–8 minutes, or until tender. Mash the mixture slightly using a potato masher.

Meanwhile, pour the stock into a separate saucepan and bring to the boil. Reduce the heat, then cover and keep at simmering point. Add the rice to the vegetables and cook for 1–2 minutes, stirring constantly, until the grains are translucent and heated through. Add 125 ml (4 fl oz/½ cup) of the simmering stock and cook, stirring constantly, until all the stock has been absorbed. Continue adding the stock, 125 ml (4 fl oz/½ cup) at a time, stirring constantly and making sure the stock has been absorbed before adding more. Cook for 20–25 minutes, or until the rice is tender and creamy; you may need slightly less or more stock.

Remove from the heat, then add the remaining butter, cheese, nutmeg and thyme. Season with freshly ground black pepper and stir thoroughly. Cover and leave for 5 minutes before serving.

carrot, spice & sour cream cake

serves 8–10

310 g (11 oz/2½ cups) self-raising
    flour
2 teaspoons ground cinnamon
1 teaspoon ground nutmeg
150 g (5½ oz/¾ cup) dark brown
    sugar
200 g (7 oz/1⅓ cups) grated carrot
4 eggs
250 g (9 oz/1 cup) sour cream
250 ml (9 fl oz/1 cup) vegetable
    oil

orange cream cheese icing

3 tablespoons cream cheese,
    softened
20 g (¾ oz) unsalted butter,
    softened
1 teaspoon grated orange zest
2 teaspoons orange juice
125 g (4½ oz/1 cup) icing
    (confectioners') sugar

Preheat the oven to 160°C (315°F/Gas 2–3). Grease a deep, 22 cm (8½ inch) round cake tin and line the base with baking paper. Sift the flour, cinnamon and nutmeg into a large bowl, then stir in the sugar and carrot until well combined.

In a bowl, beat together the eggs, sour cream and oil. Add to the flour mixture and stir until well combined. Spoon the batter into the cake tin and smooth the surface even.

Bake for 1 hour, or until a cake tester inserted into the centre of the cake comes out clean. Remove from the oven and allow to cool in the tin for 10 minutes, before turning out onto a wire rack to cool completely.

To make the orange cream cheese icing, beat the cream cheese, butter and orange zest and juice in a bowl using electric beaters until light and fluffy. Gradually add the icing sugar and beat until smooth. Spread the icing over the top of the cooled cake. Cut into slices to serve.

Without the icing, the cake will keep for 4 days, stored in a cool place in an airtight container, or can be frozen in an airtight container for up to 3 months. The iced cake will keep for 2 days, stored in a cool place in an airtight container.

farmhouse rhubarb pie

serves 6

185 g (6½ ½ oz/1½ cups) plain
  (all-purpose) flour
2 tablespoons icing
  (confectioners') sugar
125 g (4½ oz) cold unsalted butter,
  chopped
1 egg yolk, mixed with
  1 tablespoon iced water

filling

220 g (7¾ oz/1 cup) sugar, plus
  extra, for sprinkling
750 g (1 lb 10 oz/6 cups) chopped
  rhubarb
2 large apples, peeled, cored and
  chopped
2 teaspoons grated lemon zest
3 pieces of preserved ginger,
  sliced
ground cinnamon, for sprinkling
icing (confectioners') sugar, for
  dusting (optional)

Sift the flour, icing sugar and a pinch of sea salt into a large bowl. Using your fingertips, lightly rub the butter into the flour until the mixture resembles coarse breadcrumbs. Make a well in the centre. Add the egg yolk mixture to the well and mix using a flat-bladed knife until a rough dough forms. Gently gather the dough together, transfer to a lightly floured surface, then press into a round disc. Cover with plastic wrap and refrigerate for 30 minutes, or until firm.

Meanwhile, preheat the oven to 190°C (375°F/Gas 5). Grease a 20 cm (8 inch) pie plate. Roll the pastry out to a 35 cm (14 inch) circle and ease it into the pie plate, allowing the excess to hang over the edge. Refrigerate the pastry-lined dish while preparing the filling.

In a saucepan, heat the sugar and 125 ml (4 fl oz/½ cup) water for 4–5 minutes, or until syrupy. Add the rhubarb, apple, lemon zest and ginger. Cover and gently simmer for 5 minutes, or until the rhubarb is cooked but still holds its shape.

Drain off the liquid and allow the rhubarb to cool. Spoon into the pastry shell and sprinkle with the cinnamon and a little extra sugar. Fold the overhanging pastry over the filling and bake for 40 minutes, or until golden. Dust with icing sugar before serving, if desired.

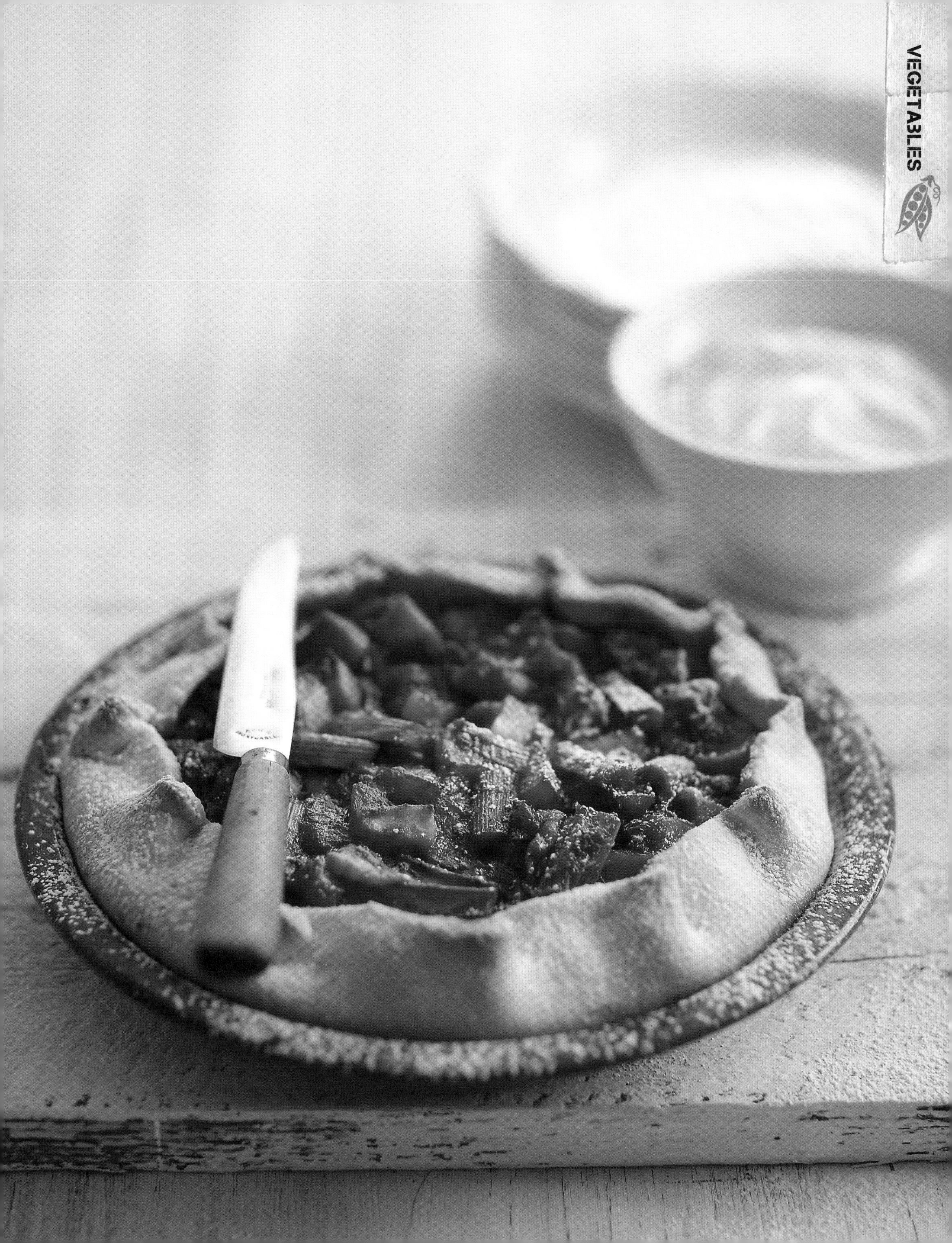

Brussels sprouts with pancetta

serves 4 as a side dish

100 g (3½ oz) pancetta, thinly sliced
4 shallots
20 g (¾ oz) butter

1 tablespoon olive oil
1 garlic clove, crushed
500 g (1 lb 2 oz) brussels sprouts, trimmed and thickly sliced

Preheat the oven grill (broiler) to high. Spread the pancetta on a baking tray lined with foil and place 8–10 cm (3¼–4 inches) under the heat. Grill for 1 minute, or until crisp, then set aside to cool.

Put the shallots in a saucepan of boiling water for 5 minutes to make them easier to peel. Remove the shallots using a slotted spoon, allow to cool slightly, then peel and cut into thick rings.

Heat the butter and olive oil in a large frying pan. Add the shallot and garlic and sauté over medium heat for 3–4 minutes, or until just starting to brown. Add the brussels sprouts and season with freshly ground black pepper. Sauté for 4–5 minutes, or until the brussels sprouts are light golden and crisp. Turn off the heat, cover and set aside for 5 minutes.

Break the pancetta into large pieces, gently toss through the vegetables and serve.

basil

Basil tastes its best when harvested before the plant flowers, so when purchasing, avoid any with flowers in evidence. Leaves should be verdantly green, slightly glossy and devoid of holes or signs of decay.

A bunch of basil should keep for 1 week in the refrigerator—trim the ends of the stalks then place in a glass of water. Place the whole bunch in a plastic bag and seal. The leaves bruise very easily so don't wash or chop them until just before you need them.

If you grow basil and have more than you can use, excess leaves can easily be frozen. Blanch them briefly in boiling water and drain. Plunge into iced water and drain again, then pat dry and freeze in airtight bags. There is no need to defrost before using.

bay leaf

Fresh leaves will keep, stored in a loosely sealed plastic bag, in the refrigerator for at least 1 week.

chives

Chives are delicate and do not last long once picked. Choose bunches with leaves that show no signs of yellowing, wilting or decay (water will cause them to start rotting). Store chives, wrapped in damp paper towels then placed in a loosely sealed plastic bag, in the refrigerator for up to 3–4 days.

coriander

Coriander does not store well, so should be used within 1–2 days or so of purchase and refrigerated in an airtight container until needed.

When purchasing, look for bunches with bright green, unblemished leaves; avoid overly limp bunches and do not purchase any that are bruised or showing signs of sliminess or yellowing.

dill

Dill is quite fragile and wilts very quickly after it is picked. To store it, spray with a fine mist of water, wrap carefully in damp paper towels then seal in a plastic bag and keep in the crisper section of the refrigerator for up to 5 days. You can also freeze dill for up to 8 weeks—it will turn an unattractive dark green colour and the flavour won't be as strong as the fresh herb, but is still preferable to using dried dill.

oregano and marjoram

As with all fresh herbs, choose oregano and marjoram that shows no signs of drooping, yellowing or drying. Stems of these herbs will store well in the refrigerator (up to 1 week) if wrapped in slightly damp paper towels then loosely sealed in a plastic bag.

lemon grass

Although you can purchase dried and powdered lemon grass, these are but pale imitations of the real thing—there really is no comparison. Choose lemon grass stalks that are plump and firm, with no signs of drying or brittleness. They will keep, stored in a tightly sealed plastic bag in the refrigerator, for 2–3 weeks.

Lemon grass can be successfully frozen. Cut off the tough green ends and wrap stalks tightly in foil and then plastic wrap. Cut from the stalk as you require lemon grass. It will lose a little of its potency but this is a preferable trade-off if the choice is between using a frozen or dried alternative.

SELECTION & STORAGE

mint

Mint owes its clean, cool flavour to the presence of the volatile oil menthol that quickly dissipates so, as is the case with most fresh herbs, avoid cutting or tearing the leaves until just before you use them.

When buying mint, choose bunches that are sprightly, with bright green leaves that show no signs of drooping or yellowing.

Fresh mint will store for 3–4 days when wrapped carefully in damp paper and loosely sealed in a plastic bag in the refrigerator.

parsley

When selecting parsley to buy, try to ensure it is young. This is a little easier to do with the flat-leaf (Italian) variety for as it ages the leaves become large, leathery and resemble celery leaves, and their flavour is coarse.

Store parsley with its stalks in a container of water in the refrigerator and with a plastic bag sealing the cup and leaves. Flat-leaf parsley can be stored wrapped in damp paper towels then loosely sealed in a plastic bag. Stored this way, parsley will keep for about 4 days.

rosemary

Rosemary is fairly robust, and not subject to the bruising or wilting of other more fragile herbs. When buying rosemary, look for sprightly, green-leafed sprigs with fresh, resinous aromas when a few are rubbed between your fingers. Old rosemary looks dried out and somewhat faded and its smell is similarly diminished.

Store fresh rosemary in an airtight container or sealed plastic bag in the refrigerator for up to 1 week.

sage

Sage can be purchased in bunches—the leaves should be fresh-looking with no signs of wilting, brown spots or bruising. Stored in the refrigerator in a sealed plastic bag for 5–6 days.

tarragon

Choose tarragon with fresh-looking, unbruised leaves that show no signs of wilting. Store tarragon, wrapped in damp paper towels, then loosely sealed in a plastic bag, in the refrigerator for up to 4 days.

thyme

Common thyme has tiny ovoid, tough, deep green leaves which are generally used whole, still attached to a branch as a sprig. Unlike most other herbs, common thyme is best added to dishes at the beginning of cooking and discarded before serving—the flavour subtly perfumes the dish whereas freshly chopped leaves tend to overpower and taste too 'green'.

When buying thyme, select bunches with a profusion of compact, green leaves with no signs of dropping or drying out. Wrap the bunch in damp paper towels and place in a loosely sealed plastic bag—it will keep for up to 1 week in the refrigerator.

CHAPTER TWO

fruit

blackberries • lemons • apples • peaches
passionfruit • mangoes • plums
cherries • figs

avocado & grapefruit salad

serves 4

2 ruby grapefruits
1 ripe avocado
200 g (7 oz) watercress sprigs

1 French shallot, finely sliced
1 tablespoon sherry vinegar
3 tablespoons olive oil

Using a small sharp knife, peel each grapefruit, taking care to remove all the white pith. Working over a bowl to catch any juices for the dressing, carefully remove the grapefruit segments by cutting between the white membrane and the flesh. Squeeze out any juice remaining in the membranes into the bowl.

Peel the avocado, cut it in half and remove the stone. Cut the flesh into 2 cm (¾ inch) wedges and place in a bowl with the grapefruit segments, watercress and shallot.

Put 1 tablespoon of the reserved grapefruit juice in a small bowl with the vinegar, olive oil and a little sea salt and freshly ground black pepper. Whisk together well, then pour the dressing over the salad and toss gently to coat. Divide among serving plates and serve immediately.

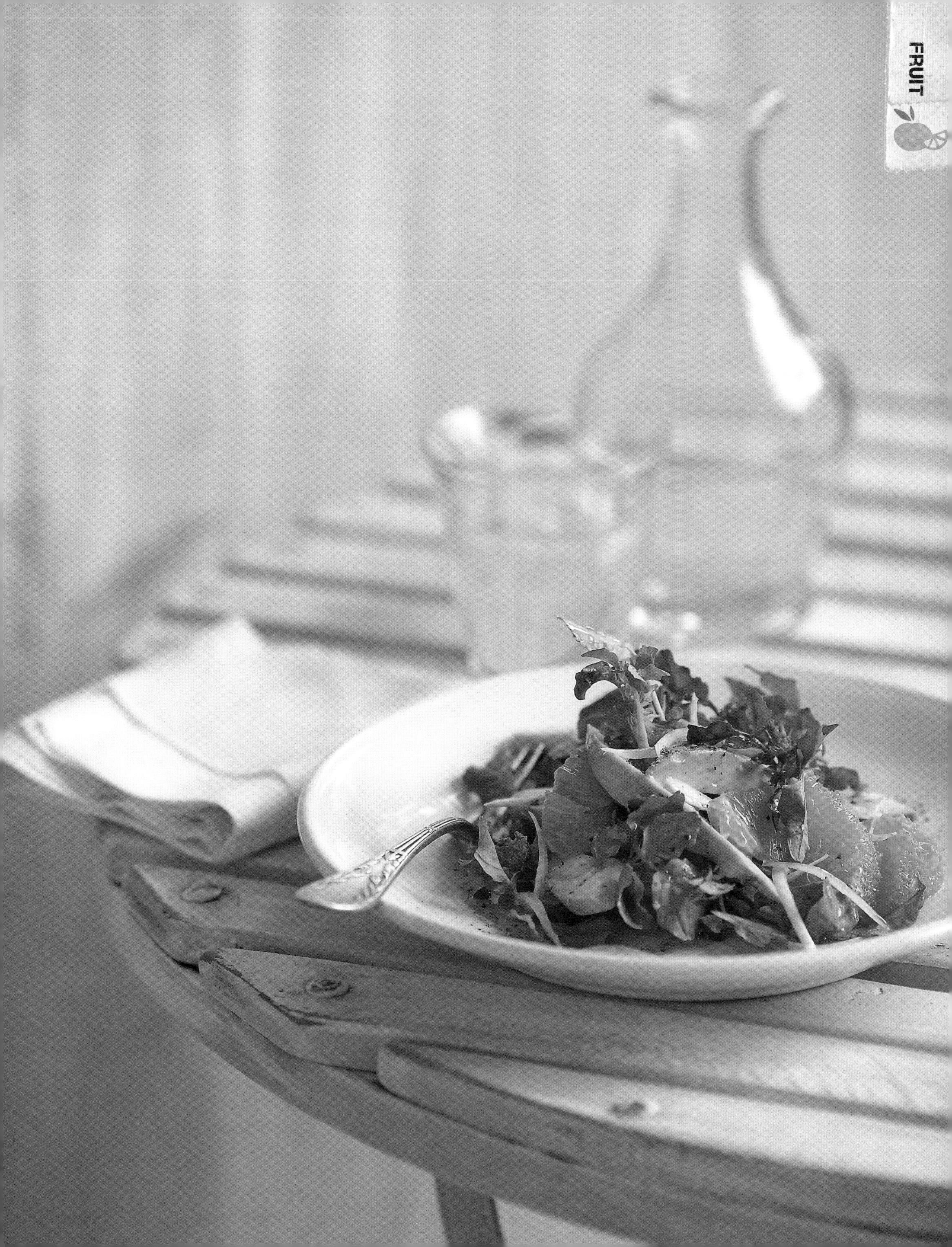

chicken with apricots & honey

serves 4

40 g (1½ oz) butter
1 teaspoon ground cinnamon
1 teaspoon ground ginger
⅛ teaspoon cayenne pepper
4 x 175 g (6 oz) chicken breasts, trimmed
1 onion, sliced
250 ml (9 fl oz/1 cup) ready-made chicken stock

6 sprigs coriander (cilantro), tied in a bunch
500 g (1 lb 2 oz or about 10) apricots, halved and stones removed
2 tablespoons honey
2 tablespoons slivered almonds, toasted, to serve (optional)
couscous, to serve

Melt the butter in a large frying pan. Add the spices, season with freshly ground black pepper and stir over low heat for about 1 minute, or until fragrant. Increase the heat to medium and add the chicken breasts. Cook for 1 minute on each side, taking care not to let the spices burn.

Add the onion and cook for 5 minutes, stirring the onion and turning the chicken occasionally. Add the stock and coriander sprigs and season to taste. Reduce the heat to low, cover and simmer for 5 minutes, turning the chicken once.

Transfer the chicken to a serving dish, cover and rest for 2–3 minutes. Put the apricots, cut side down, into the pan with the juices and drizzle with honey. Cover and simmer for 7–8 minutes, turning the apricots after 5 minutes. Remove the coriander and discard. Spoon the apricots and sauce over the chicken, scatter with almonds, if using, and serve with couscous passed separately.

warm salad of watercress, citrus & spring lamb

serves 4

This salad is spring on a plate: the zing of citrus combines with the peppery, mustardy taste of raw watercress leaves, which complements the seared lamb. For the tenderest results, try spring lamb (three to ten months old) or milk-fed lamb (generally under eight weeks of age).

dressing

1 tablespoon red wine vinegar
1 clove garlic, crushed
$\frac{1}{2}$ teaspoon honey
2 teaspoons walnut oil
$1\frac{1}{2}$ tablespoons olive oil

300g/10$\frac{1}{2}$ ounces lamb
    tenderloins
1 tablespoon olive oil
2 oranges
1 small pink grapefruit
3 large handfuls watercress,
    washed and sorted
$\frac{1}{2}$ small red onion, finely sliced

To make the dressing, put all the ingredients in a small bowl, season with salt and freshly ground black pepper, and whisk to combine.

Cut the lamb tenderloins in half and season with freshly ground black pepper. Heat the olive oil in a frying pan over high heat and cook the lamb for 3–4 minutes or until browned, turning once or twice. Season with salt and remove from the heat.

Peel the oranges and grapefruit, removing all the white pith. Holding them over a bowl to catch the juice, segment them by using a small, sharp knife to cut between the membranes. Put the segments in the bowl with the juices.

Cut the lamb diagonally into 2.5 cm (1 inch) thick slices and add to the bowl, along with the watercress and red onion. Pour the dressing over the salad and lightly toss to coat.

coriander pork with fresh pineapple

serves 4

400 g (14 oz) pork loin or fillet, trimmed
¼ pineapple
1 tablespoon vegetable oil
4 garlic cloves, chopped
4 spring onions (scallions), chopped

1 tablespoon fish sauce
1 tablespoon lime juice
a large handful of coriander (cilantro) leaves
a large handful of chopped mint
steamed rice, to serve

Partially freeze the pork until it is just firm, then slice thinly. Cut the skin off the pineapple, then cut the flesh into bite-sized pieces.

Heat the oil in a wok or heavy-based frying pan. Add the garlic and spring onion and cook over medium–high heat for 1 minute. Remove from the wok.

Heat the wok to very hot, then add the pork in batches and stir-fry for 2–3 minutes, or until just cooked.

Return the garlic, spring onion and all the pork to the wok and add the pineapple, fish sauce and lime juice. Toss together, then cook for 1 minute, or until the pineapple is heated through.

Toss the coriander and mint through and serve immediately with steamed rice.

grilled figs in prosciutto

makes 12

25 g (1 oz) unsalted butter
1 tablespoon orange juice
12 small ripe figs

12 sage leaves
6 slices prosciutto, trimmed and
  halved lengthways

Put the butter in a small heavy-based saucepan. Melt the butter over low heat, then cook for 8–10 minutes, or until the froth subsides and the milk solids appear as brown specks on the bottom of the saucepan. Strain the butter through a sieve lined with paper towels into a clean bowl, then stir in the orange juice.

Wash the figs gently and pat them dry with paper towels. Cut each fig into quarters, starting from the stem end and cutting almost to the base, then gently open out—figs will open like a flower. Put a sage leaf in the opening of each fig, then wrap a piece of prosciutto around each one, tucking the ends under the base of the fig. Arrange the figs, cut side up, in a shallow ovenproof dish and brush with the butter mixture.

Put the tray of figs under a hot grill (broiler) and cook for 1–2 minutes, or until the prosciutto is slightly crisp. Serve warm or at room temperature.

rhubarb & apple upside-down cake

serves 6–8

250 g (9 oz/1 cup) sugar

250 g (9 oz) rhubarb, chopped into 2 cm (3/4 inch) pieces

1 small apple, peeled, cored and chopped

2 eggs

40 g (1¼ oz/⅓ cup) icing (confectioners') sugar

1/2 teaspoon natural vanilla extract

100 g (3½ oz) unsalted butter, melted and cooled

125 g (4½ oz/1 cup) self-raising flour

Preheat the oven to 180°C (350°F/Gas 4). Lightly grease a deep 20 cm (8 inch) round cake tin and line the base with baking paper.

Put the sugar in a saucepan with 80 ml (2½ fl oz/⅓ cup) water and heat gently, shaking occasionally, until the sugar has dissolved. Increase the heat and cook until it turns a pale caramel colour—it will turn a deeper colour in the oven. Pour into the tin and then press the rhubarb and apple into the caramel.

Beat the eggs, icing sugar and vanilla extract in a small bowl with electric beaters until the mixture is frothy. Fold in the melted butter. Sift the flour over the top and stir (the mixture will be soft). Spoon gently over the fruit, being careful not to dislodge it.

Bake for about 45 minutes, or until set on top. Run a knife around the side of the cake and turn out very carefully onto a wire rack to cool. Be sure to do this straight away, otherwise the caramel will cool and stick to the tin. Serve warm with cream as a dessert, or cool as a teacake.

Variation: Fresh plums can be substituted for the apple and rhubarb in this recipe. The plums should be halved and cored, then sliced and pressed into the caramel in a decorative spiral pattern, or randomly. Bake the cake as for the original recipe and serve either warm or cold.

spiced baked apples

serves 4

melted butter, for brushing

4 green apples

3 tablespoons raw (demerara) sugar

3 tablespoons chopped dried figs

3 tablespoons chopped dried apricots

3 tablespoons slivered almonds

1 tablespoon apricot jam

1/4 teaspoon ground cardamom

1/4 teaspoon ground cinnamon

30 g (1 oz) unsalted butter, chopped

whipped cream, custard or ice cream, to serve (optional)

Preheat the oven to 180°C (350°F/Gas 4). Brush a square, deep baking dish with melted butter. Peel the apples and remove the cores. Gently roll each apple in the sugar. In a bowl, mix together the figs, apricots, almonds, jam and spices. Fill each apple with some of the fruit mixture. Place the apples in the baking dish and dot with pieces of butter.

Bake for 35–40 minutes, or until the apples are tender. Serve warm with whipped cream, custard or ice cream, if desired. Spiced baked apples are best prepared and baked just before serving.

apple galette

serves 4–6

1 sheet ready-made puff pastry
80 g (2¾ oz/¼ cup) apricot jam
1 cooking apple, such as granny smith
2 teaspoons raw (demerara) sugar

Preheat the oven to 210°C (415°F/Gas 6–7). Trim the corners from the pastry to make a neat 24 cm (9½ inch) circle (use a large plate as a guide if you like). Put the jam in a small saucepan and stir over low heat until melted. Strain the jam, discarding any solids, then brush over the puff pastry, leaving a 1.5 cm (⅝ inch) border.

Peel, quarter and core the apple, and cut into 2 mm (1/16 inch) thick slices. Arrange over the pastry in an overlapping circular pattern, leaving a 1.5 cm (½ inch) border around the edge. Sprinkle evenly with the sugar. Carefully place the galette on a lightly greased tray and bake for 35 minutes, or until the edge of the pastry is well browned and puffed.

SELECTION & STORAGE

apples

Apples continue to ripen once picked, so the fruit bowl is a great place to keep them if yours are slightly under-ripe.

Apples kept in cold storage eventually lose flavour, juiciness and crispness, their most desirable qualities. It is best to either buy apple varieties as they come into season, or purchase fruit from farmer's or grower's markets and roadside stalls that dot the landscape of apple-orchard territory. Buying this way may also provide an opportunity to sample some lesser-known varieties.

Favour firm, smooth and shiny-skinned apples that feel heavy for their size. Apples should still have their stalk intact and have dry, tight skin. Bruised apples deteriorate rapidly, so are best trimmed, then used immediately.

Apples slowly continue ripening after picking, so keep them in a ventilated plastic bag in the refrigerator crisper for 1 week. To store quantities of apples for out-of-season use, wrap firm fruit, individually, in tissue paper then spread on slatted wooden boxes (or similar). They need to be stored in a cool, dry, well-ventilated place where they will keep for several months (check them occasionally for signs of deterioration).

blackberries

Blackberries remain sour long after they turn black and are not truly ripe and ready to eat until they are soft. Consume them quickly, as they lose their flavour fast. Blackberries should be plump and their stems removed—attached stems are a sign that they were picked too early and may be under-ripe and tasteless.

Like all berries, blackberries can be frozen. To freeze berries so they 'free-flow' (as opposed to being frozen in a lump), spread them in a single layer on trays lined with baking paper, then freeze solid. Transfer to an airtight container or freezer bag, pressing all the air out of the bag, then seal and use within 6 months.

fig

There are hundreds of varieties of figs. All are highly perishable and range in colour from purple, brown, green to white, with flesh colour from crimson and pinkish brown to amber.

Choose figs that feel yielding but not squashy, and that have no splits, bruises, black spots, leaking or wrinkling on their skin. Ripe figs are sometimes coated with a natural, light whitish bloom; this is desirable.

Store figs on an uncovered tray or plate in the refrigerator for 2–3 days, but be sure to allow them to come to room temperature before eating, as chilling tends to dull their glorious flavour.

lemon

Choose lemons that have firm, unblemished, glossy yellow skin. Avoid buying lemons that are wrinkled, have cuts or soft spots or are still green—the flavour of the latter will not be fully developed. Avoid any fruits that are damp, as this causes mould to quickly grow and spread among other lemons that sit nearby.

Lemons will store for up to 2 weeks in the refrigerator or up to 1 week at cool room temperature.

passionfruit

Passionfruit grows on a vine, from which it drops when the fruit is ready. Purple passionfruit should be avoided if the skin is smooth, as they will be too tart to enjoy—when ripe their skin thins a little and becomes wrinkled.

Ripe passionfruit will keep at cool room temperature for about 1 week and up to 3 weeks if refrigerated. Both passionfruit pulp and the strained juice can be frozen.

pears

Pears are picked when mature but still hard, then transferred to cool storage to cure for a period (the length of time here depends upon variety) and then, finally, bought to room temperature to complete ripening. During ripening, the starches are converted to sugars, and the pear, unusually, ripens from the inside out.

When allowed to fully tree-ripen, pears are fit to eat for a few days only, after which their flesh turns dry and mealy. Perhaps this is why, before the days of commercial cool storage, Ralph Waldo Emerson declared that, 'There are only ten minutes in the life of a pear when it is perfect to eat'.

To tell if a pear is ripe, it should give slightly when pressed (use your thumb) at the base of the 'neck'. Some varieties will also smell a little fragrant. Asian pears are the exception to the above rules as they are picked when ready to eat.

parmesan pears

serves 6

3 ripe firm pears, such as packham or beurre bosc

40 g (1½ oz) unsalted butter

6 thin slices of pancetta, finely chopped

2 spring onions (scallions), finely sliced

60 g (2¼ oz/¾ cup) fresh white breadcrumbs

4 tablespoons grated parmesan cheese

Heat the oven grill (broiler) to medium–high. Cut the pears in half lengthways and remove the cores. Melt the butter in a frying pan. Brush the pears with a little of the melted butter and place, cut side up, on a baking tray or grill tray. Grill for 4 minutes, or until starting to brown on top.

Add the pancetta and spring onion to the remaining butter in the pan. Sauté over medium heat for 3 minutes, or until the spring onion is soft but not brown. Stir in the breadcrumbs and some freshly ground black pepper to taste.

Spoon the pancetta mixture into the pear cavities, sprinkle with the parmesan and grill for 3 minutes, or until the cheese is golden brown. Serve warm as a starter, or as an accompaniment to roast chicken.

blackberry & pear strudel

serves 6–8

Thank goodness for ready-made filo pastry! Without it, few would attempt making a strudel. This version branches out from the traditional apple and raisin or cherry and cream cheese filling by combining citrus-infused pears with blackberries, almonds and sultanas.

120 g (4¼ oz) unsalted butter

½ teaspoon natural vanilla extract

4 pears, peeled, cored and chopped

1 teaspoon orange zest, finely grated

½ lemon, juiced

5 sheets filo pastry

120 g (4¼ oz/1½ cups) fresh breadcrumbs

200 g (7 oz/1½ cups) blackberries

50 g (1¾ oz/½ cup) toasted flaked almonds

60 g (2¼ oz/½ cup) sultanas

165 g (5¾ oz/¾ cup) caster (superfine) sugar

icing (confectioners') sugar, for dusting

custard or vanilla ice cream, to serve

Preheat the oven to 180°C (350°F/Gas 4) and line a baking sheet with baking paper. Melt 100 g (3½ oz) of the butter with the vanilla.

Melt the remaining butter in a frying pan and sauté the pear over low heat for 5 minutes, or until tender. Transfer to a large bowl with the orange zest and lemon juice. Toss lightly to combine.

Lay a sheet of filo pastry on a flat surface. Brush the melted butter over the pastry and sprinkle lightly with breadcrumbs. Cover with another sheet of pastry and repeat the process until you have used all the pastry. Sprinkle with the remaining breadcrumbs.

Add the blackberries, almonds, sultanas and caster sugar to the pear mixture and toss gently to combine. Shape the filling into a log along one long edge of the pastry, leaving a 5 cm (2 inch) border. Fold in the sides, then roll up and place, seam side down, on the prepared baking sheet. Brush with the remaining melted butter and bake for 40 minutes, or until golden brown. Dust with icing sugar and serve with custard or vanilla ice cream.

blueberry pancakes

makes 12

250 g (9 oz/2 cups) plain
   (all-purpose) flour

2 teaspoons baking powder

1 teaspoon bicarbonate of soda
   (baking soda)

75 g (2½ oz/⅓ cup) sugar

2 eggs

80 g (2¾ oz) unsalted butter,
   melted

310 ml (10¾ fl oz/1¼ cups) milk

310 g (11 oz/2 cups) blueberries,
   fresh or frozen, plus extra to serve

honey and plain yoghurt, to serve

Sift the flour, baking powder and bicarbonate of soda into a large bowl. Add the sugar and make a well in the centre. Add the eggs, melted butter and milk to the dry ingredients, stirring just to combine (add more milk if you prefer a thinner batter).

Gently fold the blueberries into the batter (leave some for serving). Heat a frying pan and brush lightly with melted butter or oil. Drop tablespoons of batter into the pan and cook over low heat until bubbles appear and pop on the surface.

Turn the pancakes over and cook the other side (these pancakes can be difficult to handle so take care when turning). Transfer to a plate and cover with a cloth to keep warm while you cook the rest of the batter. Serve warm with extra blueberries, plain yoghurt and a drizzle of honey.

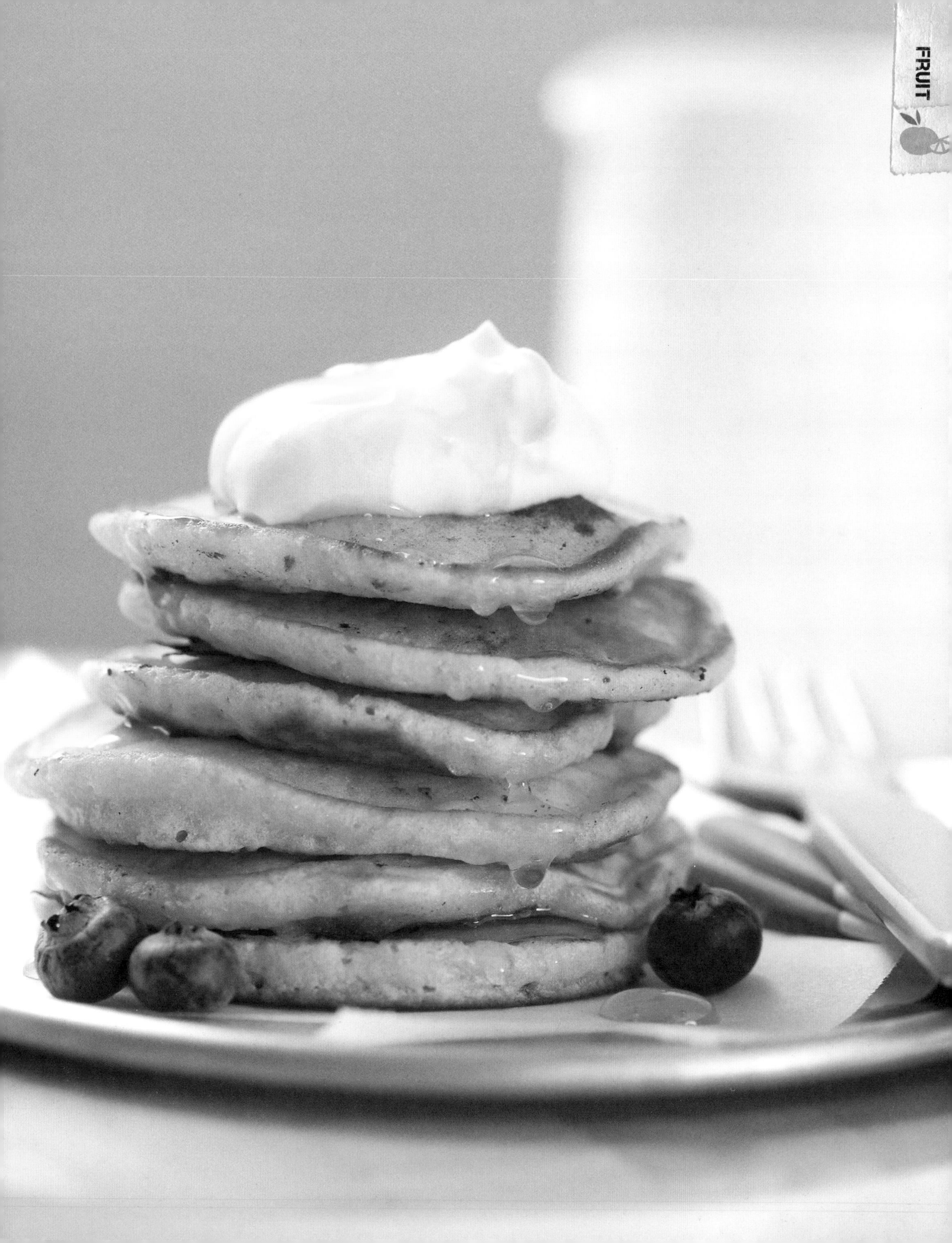

cherry & cream cheese strudel

serves 8

250 g (9 oz/1 cup) cream cheese, at room temperature

100 ml (3½ fl oz) pouring (whipping) cream

1 tablespoon brandy or cherry brandy

1 teaspoon natural vanilla extract

100 g (3½ oz/scant ½ cup) caster (superfine) sugar

4 tablespoons dry breadcrumbs

4 tablespoons ground almonds

10 sheets of filo pastry

75 g (2½ oz) unsalted butter, melted

425 g (15 oz) cherries, pitted

icing (confectioners') sugar, for dusting

Preheat the oven to 200°C (400°F/Gas 6). Lightly grease a large baking tray. Put the cream cheese, cream, brandy, vanilla and 3 tablespoons of the sugar in a bowl and beat using electric beaters until smooth.

In another bowl, mix together the breadcrumbs, almonds and remaining sugar. Lay a sheet of filo pastry on a work surface and cover the remaining sheets with a damp tea towel (dish towel) so they don't dry out. Brush the pastry with some of the melted butter and sprinkle with some of the breadcrumb mixture. Lay another sheet of pastry on top, brush with more butter and sprinkle with more breadcrumbs. Repeat with the remaining filo and breadcrumbs.

Spread the cream cheese mixture evenly over the pastry, leaving a 4 cm (1½ inch) border all around. Arrange the cherries over the cream cheese, then brush some melted butter over the pastry border.

Roll the pastry in from one long side, folding in the ends as you roll. Form into a firm roll and place on the baking tray, seam side down. Brush all over with the remaining butter.

Bake for 10 minutes, then reduce the oven temperature to 180°C (350°F/Gas 4) and bake for a further 30 minutes, or until the pastry is crisp and golden. Remove from the oven and leave to cool on a wire rack for a few minutes. To serve, dust liberally with icing sugar and cut into slices using a sharp serrated knife. Serve warm. Cherry and cream cheese strudel is best eaten the day it is made.

sponge cake with strawberries & cream

serves 6

30 g (1 oz) butter, melted

60 g (2¼ oz/½ cup) plain (all-purpose) flour

60 g (2¼ oz/½ cup) cornflour (cornstarch)

2 teaspoons cream of tartar

1 teaspoon bicarbonate of soda (baking soda)

4 eggs

170 g (6 oz/¾ cup) caster (superfine) sugar

2 tablespoons hot milk

300 ml (10½ fl oz) pouring (whipping) cream

1 tablespoon icing (confectioners') sugar, plus extra to dust

2 tablespoons strawberry jam

500 g (1 lb 2 oz) strawberries, hulled and sliced in half

Preheat the oven to 180°C (350°F/Gas 4). Grease two 20 cm (8 inch) round cake tins with the melted butter. Line the bases with baking paper. Dust the sides of the tins with a little flour, shaking out any excess.

Sift the flour, cornflour, cream of tartar and bicarbonate of soda into a bowl, then repeat twice.

Whisk the eggs and sugar in a bowl for 5 minutes, or until pale and thick. Fold in the flour mixture and the hot milk until they are just combined. Do not overmix.

Divide the mixture evenly between the two tins. Bake for 18–20 minutes, or until golden. Leave in the tins for 5 minutes, then turn out onto a wire rack to cool.

Whip the cream and icing sugar in a bowl until fluffy. Place a sponge cake on a plate and spread with jam. Top with half the cream and half of the strawberries.

Cover with the second sponge. Spread the remaining cream over the top and top with the remaining strawberries. Dust with icing sugar to serve.

amaretti-stuffed peaches

serves 6

6 ripe peaches
60 g (2¼ oz) amaretti biscuits,
  crushed
1 egg yolk
2 tablespoons caster (superfine)
  sugar, plus extra, for sprinkling

3 tablespoons ground almonds
2 teaspoons amaretto
3 tablespoons white wine
20 g (¾ oz) unsalted butter,
  chopped

Preheat the oven to 180°C (350°F/Gas 4). Lightly grease a 30 x 25 cm (12 x 10 inch) baking dish.

Cut each peach in half and remove the stones; if the peaches are cling-stone, carefully use a paring knife to cut around and remove the stone. Using a paring knife, scoop a little of the flesh out from each peach to create a slight cavity. Chop the scooped-out flesh and place it in a small bowl with the crushed biscuits, egg yolk, sugar, ground almonds and amaretto. Mix together well.

Spoon some of the stuffing mixture into each peach, then place the peaches in the baking dish, cut side up. Sprinkle with the wine and a little extra sugar. Dot with the butter and bake for 20–25 minutes, or until golden. Serve warm.

Variation: When in season, you can also use ripe apricots or nectarines for this recipe.

sweet grape flatbread

serves 6-8

100 g (3½ oz/¾ cup) raisins
90 ml (3 fl oz) sweet marsala
150 ml (5 fl oz) milk
115 g (4 oz/½ cup) caster
   (superfine) sugar
2 teaspoons active dried yeast

300 g (10½ oz/scant 2½ cups)
   plain (all-purpose) flour, plus
   extra, for dusting
400 g (14 oz/2¼ cups) black
   seedless grapes

Put the raisins in a bowl and pour the marsala over. Set aside.

Warm the milk and pour into a small bowl. Stir in 1 teaspoon of the
sugar, sprinkle the yeast over and set aside in a draught-free place for
10 minutes, or until foamy. Put the flour, 4 tablespoons of the sugar and
a pinch of sea salt in a bowl and mix together. Add the yeast mixture
and mix using a wooden spoon until a rough dough forms.

Turn out onto a lightly floured surface and knead for 6–8 minutes, or
until smooth and elastic. Add a little more flour or a few drops of warm
water if necessary to give a soft, but not sticky, dough.

Place the dough in a large oiled bowl, turning to coat in the oil. Cover
with plastic wrap and leave to rise in a draught-free place for 1 hour,
or until doubled in size.

Drain the raisins and squeeze them dry. Lightly dust a baking tray with
flour. Gently deflate the dough using a lightly floured fist, then divide
in half. Shape each half into a flattened round about 20 cm (8 inches) in
diameter and place one round on the baking tray. Scatter half the grapes
and half the raisins over the dough, then cover with the second round
of dough. Scatter the remaining grapes and raisins over the top. Cover
loosely with a tea towel (dish towel) and leave in a draught-free place for
1 hour, or until doubled in size.

Meanwhile, preheat the oven to 180°C (350°F/Gas 4). Sprinkle the dough
with the remaining sugar and bake for 40–50 minutes, or until golden.
Serve warm or at room temperature, cut into thick slices.

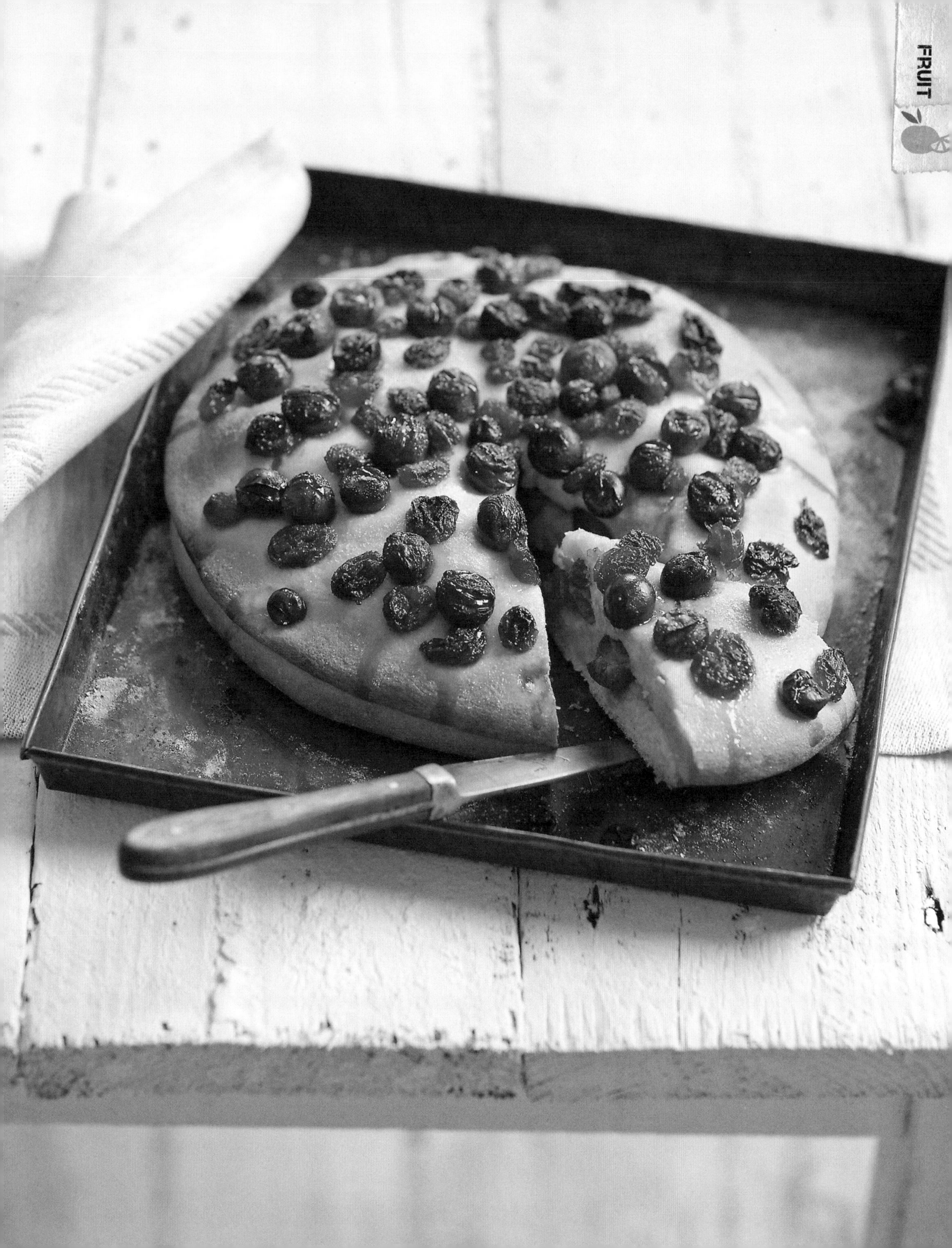

hot passionfruit soufflé

serves 4

2 egg yolks

125 g (4½ oz/½ cup) passionfruit
pulp (from about 10 passionfruit)

2 tablespoons lemon juice

90 g (3¼ oz/¾ cup) icing
(confectioners') sugar, plus extra
for dusting

6 egg whites

passionfruit sauce

60 ml (2 fl oz/¼ cup) passionfruit
pulp (from about 4 passionfruit)

2 tablespoons caster (superfine)
sugar

Preheat the oven to 210°C (415°F/Gas 6–7). Place a collar of baking paper to come about 3 cm (11/4 inches) above the outside of four small 125 ml (4 fl oz/½ cup) ramekins. Tie collars securely with string. Lightly grease the ramekins (including the paper) and sprinkle with caster sugar; shake out any excess. Combine the egg yolks, pulp, lemon juice and half the icing sugar in a large bowl. Whisk until well combined.

Using electric beaters, whisk the egg whites in a separate bowl until soft peaks form. Gradually add the remaining icing sugar, beating well after each addition. Using a large metal spoon, fold the egg white mixture, in batches, into the passionfruit mixture. Divide the mixture among the four ramekins. Using a flat-bladed knife, cut through the mixture in a circular motion 2 cm (¾ inch) from the edge.

Put the ramekins on a large baking tray and bake for 20–25 minutes or until the soufflé is well-risen and cooked through.

To make the passionfruit sauce, combine the passionfruit pulp and the sugar in a small bowl and stir until the sugar has dissolved.

To serve, cut the collars from the dishes and serve the soufflés immediately, drizzled with passionfruit sauce and dusted with sifted icing sugar.

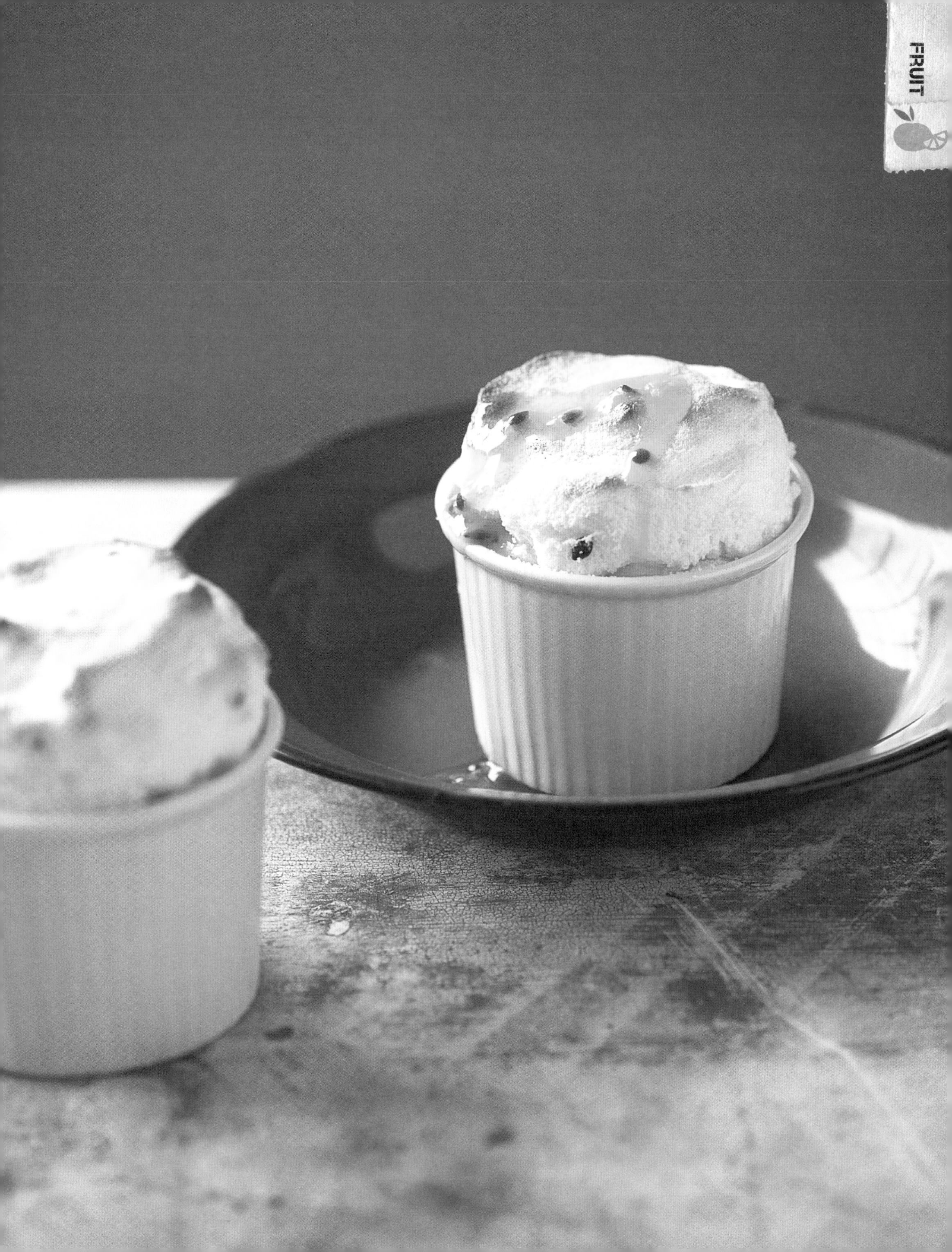

mango & passionfruit pies

makes 6

400 g (14 oz/3¼ cups) plain
   (all-purpose) flour
165 g (5¾ oz/1⅓ cups) icing
   (confectioners') sugar
200 g (7 oz) cold unsalted
   butter, chopped
2 egg yolks, mixed with
   2 tablespoons iced water
1 egg, lightly beaten
icing (confectioners') sugar,
   for dusting
whipped cream, to serve

filling

60 ml (2 fl oz/¼ cup) strained
   passionfruit pulp
1 tablespoon custard powder or
   instant vanilla pudding mix
3 ripe mangoes (900 g/2 lb),
   peeled, sliced and chopped
80 g (2¾ oz/⅓ cup) caster
   (superfine) sugar

Sift the flour and icing sugar into a large bowl. Using your fingertips, lightly rub in the butter until the mixture resembles coarse breadcrumbs. Make a well in the centre, then add the egg yolks to the well. Mix using a flat-bladed knife until a rough dough forms. Turn out onto a lightly floured work surface, then gently press together into a ball. Form into a flat disc, cover with plastic wrap and refrigerate for 30 minutes.

Grease six 10 x 8 x 3 cm (4 x 3¼ x 1¼ inch) fluted, loose-based flan (tart) tins or round pie dishes. Roll out two-thirds of the chilled pastry between two sheets of baking paper until 3 mm (⅛ inch) thick. Cut out six bases to fit the prepared tins. Gently press them into the tins and trim the edges. Refrigerate for 30 minutes.

Meanwhile, preheat the oven to 190°C (375°F/Gas 5). To make the filling, put the passionfruit pulp and custard powder in a small saucepan and mix together well.

Stir over medium heat for 2–3 minutes, or until the mixture has thickened. Remove from the heat, then stir in the mango and sugar.

Roll out the remaining pastry between two sheets of baking paper until 3 mm (⅛ inch) thick. Cut out six pie lids. Re-roll the pastry trimmings and cut into shapes for decoration.

Divide the filling among the pastry cases and brush the edges with beaten egg. Top with the pastry lids and press the edges to seal. Trim the edges and decorate the tops with the pastry shapes. Brush with beaten egg and dust with icing sugar.

Bake for 20–25 minutes, or until the pastry is golden. Remove from the oven and leave to cool in the tins. Serve warm or at room temperature with whipped cream. Mango and passionfruit pies are best eaten the day they are made.

plum cobbler

serves 6

750 g (1 lb 10 oz) plums
4 tablespoons sugar
1 teaspoon natural vanilla extract
whipped cream, to serve (optional)

topping

125 g (4½ oz/1 cup) self-raising flour
60 g (2¼ oz) cold unsalted butter, chopped
3 tablespoons soft brown sugar
3 tablespoons milk
1 tablespoon caster (superfine) sugar
icing (confectioners') sugar, for dusting

Preheat the oven to 200°C (400°F/Gas 6). Cut the plums into quarters and remove the stones. Put the plums, sugar and 2 tablespoons water in a saucepan and bring to the boil, stirring until the sugar has dissolved. Reduce the heat, then cover and simmer for 2 minutes, or until the plums are tender (some varieties will cook more quickly than others). Remove the skins if you wish, then stir in the vanilla. Spoon the mixture into a 750 ml (26 fl oz/3 cup) baking dish.

To make the topping, sift the flour into a large bowl. Using your fingertips, lightly rub in the butter until the mixture resembles fine breadcrumbs. Stir in the brown sugar. Add 2 tablespoons of the milk and mix using a flat-bladed knife until a soft dough forms, adding more milk if necessary.

Turn out onto a lightly floured surface and gather together to form a smooth dough. Roll out until 1 cm (½ inch) thick and cut into rounds using a 4 cm (1½ inch) cutter. Overlap the rounds around the side of the baking dish, over the filling. Lightly brush with the remaining milk and sprinkle with the caster sugar.

Set the dish on a baking tray and bake for 30 minutes, or until the topping is golden and cooked through. Serve hot or at room temperature, dusted with icing sugar and with whipped cream, if desired. Plum cobbler is best eaten the day it is made.

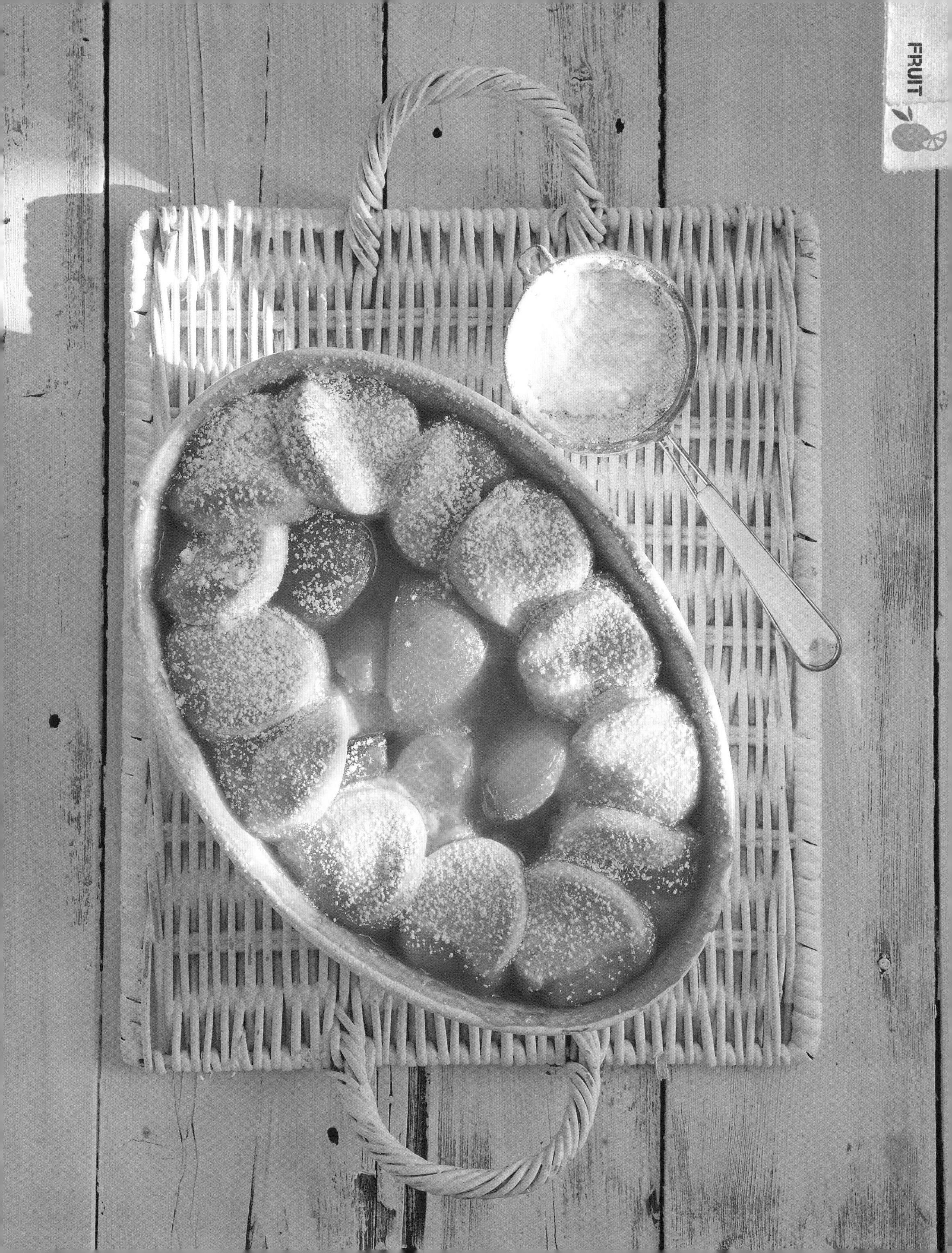

sticky orange & passionfruit pudding

serves 6

375 g (13 oz/3 cups) plain (all-purpose) flour

1½ teaspoons baking powder

200 g (7 oz) cold unsalted butter, chopped

45 g (1½ oz/½ cup) desiccated coconut

300 ml (3½ fl oz) pouring (whipping) cream

160 g (5½ oz/½ cup) orange marmalade

2 tablespoons passionfruit pulp cream, ice cream or custard, to serve

passionfruit syrup

125 ml (4 fl oz/½ cup) orange juice

170 g (6 oz/¾ cup) caster (superfine) sugar

60 ml (2 fl oz/¼ cup) passionfruit pulp

Sift the flour, baking powder and a pinch of salt into a large bowl. Using your fingertips, lightly rub in the butter until the mixture resembles fine breadcrumbs. Stir in the coconut. Using a flat-bladed knife, mix in most of the cream, adding just enough to form a soft dough.

Turn out onto a lightly floured work surface, then knead briefly. Roll the dough out between two sheets of baking paper to make a 25 x 40 cm (10 x 16 inch) rectangle.

Spread the marmalade over the dough and drizzle with the passionfruit pulp. Roll up lengthways into a log. Cover with plastic wrap and refrigerate for 20 minutes, or until firm.

Meanwhile, preheat the oven to 180°C (350°F/Gas 4). Grease an 18 cm (7 inch) round, deep cake tin and line the base with baking paper. Cut the chilled dough into 2 cm (¾ inch) rounds and arrange half of them over the base of the prepared tin. Place a second layer over the gaps where the bottom slices join. Put the cake tin on a baking tray.

Put all the passionfruit syrup ingredients in a saucepan with 60 ml (2 fl oz/¼ cup) water. Stir over low heat, without boiling, until the sugar has dissolved. Bring to the boil, then pour the syrup over the pudding.

Bake for 50 minutes, or until a cake tester inserted into the centre of the pudding comes out clean. Remove from the oven and leave in the tin for 15 minutes, before very carefully turning out into a serving dish. Serve hot, with cream, ice cream or custard. Sticky orange and passionfruit pudding is best eaten the day it is made.

queen of puddings

serves 6-8

500 ml (17 fl oz/2 cups) milk
50 g (1¾ oz) unsalted butter
140 g (5 oz/1¾ cups) fresh white
  breadcrumbs
1 tablespoon caster (superfine)
  sugar
finely grated zest of 1 orange
5 egg yolks
whipped cream, to serve (optional)

topping
210 g (7½ oz/⅔ cup) orange
  marmalade
5 egg whites
115 g (4 oz/½ cup) caster
  (superfine) sugar

Preheat the oven to 180°C (350°F/Gas 4). Lightly grease a 1.25 litre (44 fl oz/5 cup) square or rectangular baking dish. Put the milk and butter in a small saucepan and stir over low heat until the butter has melted. In a large bowl, mix together the breadcrumbs, sugar and orange zest. Stir in the milk mixture and leave to stand for 10 minutes. Lightly whisk the egg yolks, then stir into the breadcrumb mixture. Spoon into the baking dish and bake for 25–30 minutes, or until firm to the touch. Remove from the oven.

To make the topping, put the marmalade in a saucepan and melt over low heat. Spread evenly over the hot pudding. In a clean, dry bowl, beat the egg whites using electric beaters until stiff peaks form. Gradually add the sugar, whisking until the mixture is stiff and glossy and the sugar has dissolved. Spoon the meringue evenly over the pudding and bake for a further 12–15 minutes, or until the meringue is golden.

Serve warm or at room temperature, with whipped cream, if desired. Queen of puddings is best eaten the day it is made.

real lemon pie

serves 8

filling

- 4 thin-skinned lemons
- 460 g (1 lb/2 cups) caster (superfine) sugar
- 4 eggs, lightly beaten

- 310 g (11 oz/2½ cups) plain (all-purpose) flour
- 80 g (2¾ oz/⅓ cup) caster (superfine) sugar
- 225 g (8 oz) cold unsalted butter, chopped
- 2–3 tablespoons iced water
- milk, for brushing
- pouring (whipping) cream, to serve (optional)

Start making the filling a day ahead. Wash the lemons well, then dry. Peel two lemons, removing all the white pith with a small, sharp knife, then slice the flesh very thinly, removing any seeds. Leave the other two lemons unpeeled and slice very thinly, removing any seeds. Place in a bowl with the sugar and stir until the lemon slices are coated. Cover and leave to stand overnight.

Sift the flour and a pinch of salt into a large bowl, then stir in the sugar. Using your fingertips, lightly rub in the butter until the mixture resembles breadcrumbs. Make a well in the centre and gradually add most of the iced water to the well, mixing with a flat-bladed knife until a rough dough forms, adding a little extra iced water if necessary.

Turn out onto a lightly floured work surface, then gently gather the dough together. Divide in half and roll each portion into a 30 cm (12 inch) circle. Cover with plastic wrap and refrigerate for 30 minutes.

Meanwhile, preheat the oven to 180°C (350°F/Gas 4). Lightly grease a 23 cm (9 inch) pie dish that is at least 3 cm (1¼ inches) deep. Roll one sheet of pastry around the rolling pin, then lift and ease it into the pie dish, gently pressing to fit the side. Cover all the pastry with plastic wrap and refrigerate for 20 minutes.

Meanwhile, finish preparing the filling. Measure out 750 ml (26 fl oz/3 cups) of the lemon slices and liquid. Place in a bowl with the beaten eggs, stirring to mix well.

Spoon the mixture into the chilled pastry case, then cover with the pastry circle, trimming the pastry and crimping the edges to seal. Re-roll the pastry scraps and cut out decorative shapes. Place on top of the pie and brush with milk.

Bake for 50–55 minutes, or until the pastry is golden brown. Remove from the oven and allow to cool slightly. Serve straight from the dish, with cream for drizzling over, if desired. Real lemon pie is best eaten the day it is made.

preserved lemons

fills a 2 litre (70 fl oz/8 cup) jar

8-12 small thin-skinned lemons

315 g (11 oz/1 cup) rock salt

750 ml (26 fl oz/3 cups) lemon juice (10-12 lemons should yield this amount of juice)

½ teaspoon black peppercorns

1 bay leaf

olive oil, for covering

Scrub the lemons under warm running water with a soft brush to remove the wax coating, if necessary. Starting from the top and cutting almost to the base, cut the lemons into quarters, taking care not to cut all the way through. Gently open each lemon, remove any visible seeds and pack 1 tablespoon of the rock salt inside each lemon.

Push the lemons back into shape and pack tightly into a 2 litre (70 fl oz/8 cup) sterilised jar with a tight-fitting lid. The lemons should be firmly packed and fill the jar (depending on their size, you may not need all 12).

Add 250 ml (9 fl oz/1 cup) of the lemon juice, the peppercorns, bay leaf and remaining rock salt to the jar. Fill the jar to the top with the remaining lemon juice. Seal and leave in a cool, dark place for 6 weeks, inverting the jar each week to dissolve the salt. The liquid will be cloudy initially, but will clear by the fourth week.

To test if the lemons are preserved, cut through the centre of one of the lemon quarters. If the pith is still white, the lemons aren't quite ready. In this case, re-seal and leave for another week before testing again. The lemons should be soft-skinned and the pith translucent.

Once the lemons are preserved, cover the brine with a layer of olive oil. Replace the oil each time you remove some of the lemon pieces so that the lemons remain covered with oil. Refrigerate after opening.

raspberry jam

fills six 250 ml (9 fl oz/1 cup) jars

1.5 kg (3 lb 5 oz) raspberries
4 tablespoons lemon juice
1.5 kg (3 lb 5 oz) sugar

Put the raspberries and lemon juice in a large heavy-based saucepan. Gently cook over low heat for 10 minutes, or until the raspberries have softened, stirring occasionally.

Meanwhile, warm the sugar by spreading it in a large baking dish and heating it in a 120°C (250°F/Gas ½) oven for 10 minutes, stirring occasionally. Add the sugar to the pan and stir, without boiling, for 5 minutes, or until the sugar has completely dissolved.

Put two small plates in the freezer. Bring the jam to the boil and boil for 20 minutes, then start testing for setting point by placing a little of the hot jam on a chilled plate. When setting point is reached, a skin will form on the surface and the jam will wrinkle when you push it with your finger. If the jam doesn't set, keep cooking and testing until it does—this may take up to 40 minutes.

Allow to cool for 5 minutes, then skim off any impurities that have risen to the surface. Pour into hot sterilised jars and seal. Allow to cool completely, then label and date each jar. Store in a cool, dark place for 10–12 months. Once opened, raspberry jam will keep in the refrigerator for up to 4 weeks.

CHAPTER THREE

meat, poultry & seafood

beef • lamb • pork • veal • duck
chicken • salmon • prawns

lamb pilaff

serves 4

1 large eggplant (aubergine), cut into 1 cm (½ inch) cubes
125 ml (4 fl oz/½ cup) olive oil
1 large onion, finely chopped
½ teaspoon ground cinnamon
1 teaspoon ground cumin
½ teaspoon ground coriander
300 g (10½ oz/1½ cups) long-grain white rice
500 ml (17 fl oz/2 cups) chicken or vegetable stock
2 tomatoes, cut into wedges
3 tablespoons toasted pistachios
2 tablespoons currants
2 tablespoons chopped coriander (cilantro)

meatballs

500 g (1 lb 2 oz) minced (ground) lamb
½ teaspoon ground allspice
½ teaspoon ground cinnamon
1 teaspoon ground cumin
½ teaspoon ground coriander
2 tablespoons olive oil

Put the eggplant in a colander, sprinkle with salt and leave for 1 hour. Rinse, drain well, then pat dry with paper towels. Heat 2 tablespoons of the olive oil in a large, deep, frying pan, add the eggplant and cook over medium heat for 10 minutes. Remove and drain on paper towels.

Heat the remaining olive oil in the pan, add the onion and sauté for 5 minutes, or until softened. Stir in the ground spices, then add the rice and stir to coat. Pour in the stock, season with sea salt and freshly ground black pepper and bring to the boil. Reduce the heat and simmer, covered, for 15 minutes.

Meanwhile, make the meatballs. Put the lamb in a bowl with the ground spices. Season with sea salt and freshly ground black pepper and mix well. Roll the mixture into small balls the size of walnuts.

Heat the olive oil in a frying pan and cook the meatballs in batches over medium heat for 5 minutes, turning often to brown all over. Drain on paper towels. Add the tomato wedges to the frying pan and cook for 3–5 minutes, or until softened. Stir the eggplant, pistachios, currants and meatballs through the rice. Serve the pilaff with the tomato wedges, sprinkled with the coriander.

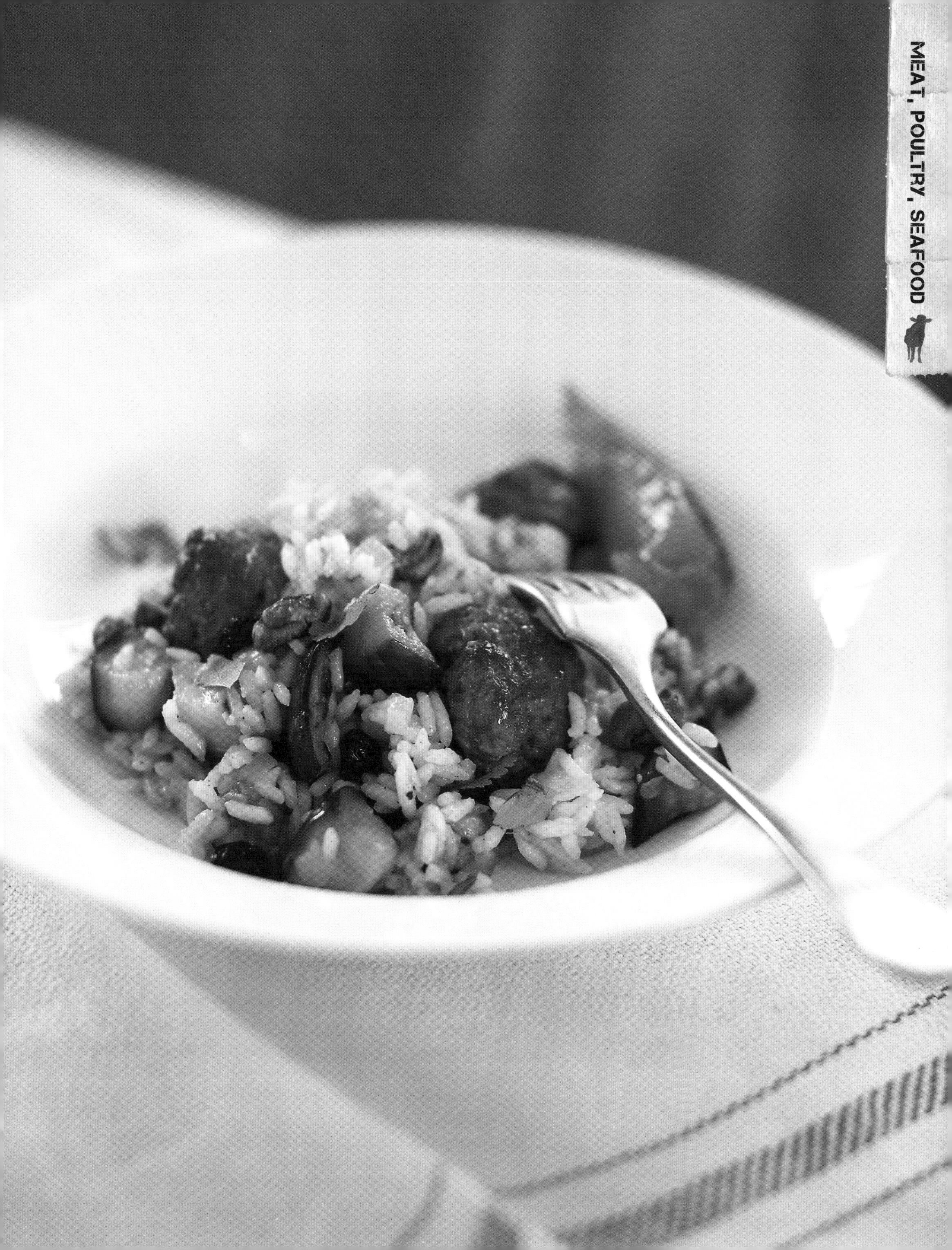

rack of lamb with mustard crust & roasted vegetables

serves 4

80 ml (2½ fl oz/⅓ cup) olive oil

½ brown onion, finely diced

1 garlic clove, finely chopped

50 g (1¾ oz/½ cup) dry breadcrumbs

1 teaspoon chopped sage

1 tablespoon dijon mustard

1 tablespoon seeded mustard

1 egg yolk

2 lamb racks, each with 6 cutlets, trimmed

12 garlic cloves, unpeeled

2 carrots, sliced diagonally

1 red capsicum (pepper), cut into thick strips

1 red onion, cut into 8 wedges

2 zucchini (courgettes), sliced diagonally

175 g (6 oz/1 bunch) asparagus, cut in half, diagonally

1 tablespoon balsamic vinegar

Put a small, heavy-based saucepan over medium heat and add 1 tablespoon of the oil with the onion and garlic. Cook for 2 minutes, or until softened. Remove from the heat, place into a bowl and cool slightly. Combine with the breadcrumbs, sage, mustards, egg yolk, and season with salt. Spread this mixture across the rack of lamb to form a thick crust. Refrigerate until ready to use.

Preheat the oven to 200°C (400°F/Gas 6). Place the lamb onto a baking tray. Put 2 tablespoons of the oil, garlic, vegetables and 1 teaspoon salt into another baking dish and toss well to coat. Place both the trays into the oven for 30–40 minutes. Stir the vegetables every 10 minutes.

The lamb is ready when the crust is golden and the lamb is firm to touch. Remove the lamb and rest for 10 minutes. Reserve the pan juices. Leave the vegetables in the oven for a further 10 minutes, or until golden. Heat the lamb pan juices with the balsamic vinegar, remaining olive oil and a pinch of salt. Slice the lamb and serve with the roasted vegetables and sauce.

osso buco alla milanese

serves 4

Osso buco is a milanese dish and, traditionally, tomatoes are not used in the cooking of northern italy. The absence of the robust tomato allows the more delicate flavour of the gremolata to feature in this classic osso buco.

12 pieces veal shank, about 4 cm (1½ inches) thick
plain (all-purpose) flour, seasoned with salt and pepper
60 ml (¼ cup) olive oil
60 g (2¼ oz) butter
1 garlic clove
250 ml (1 cup) dry white wine
1 bay leaf or lemon leaf
pinch of allspice
pinch of ground cinnamon

gremolata
2 teaspoons grated lemon zest
6 tablespoons finely chopped parsley
1 garlic clove, finely chopped

thin lemon wedges

Tie each piece of veal shank around its girth to secure the flesh, then dust with the seasoned flour. Heat the oil, butter and garlic in a large heavy saucepan big enough to hold the shanks in a single layer. Put the shanks in the pan and cook for 12–15 minutes until well browned. Arrange the shanks, standing them up in a single layer, pour in the wine and add the bay leaf, allspice and cinnamon. Cover the saucepan.

Cook at a low simmer for 15 minutes, then add 125 ml (½ cup) warm water. Continue cooking, covered, for about 45 minutes to 1 hour (the timing will depend on the age of the veal) until the meat is tender and you can cut it with a fork. Check the volume of liquid once or twice and add more warm water as needed. Transfer the veal to a plate and keep warm. Discard the garlic clove and bay leaf.

To make the gremolata, mix together the lemon zest, parsley and garlic. Increase the heat under the saucepan and stir for 1–2 minutes until the sauce is thick, scraping up any bits off the bottom of the saucepan as you stir. Stir in the gremolata. Season with salt and pepper if necessary and return the veal to the sauce. Heat through, then serve with the lemon wedges.

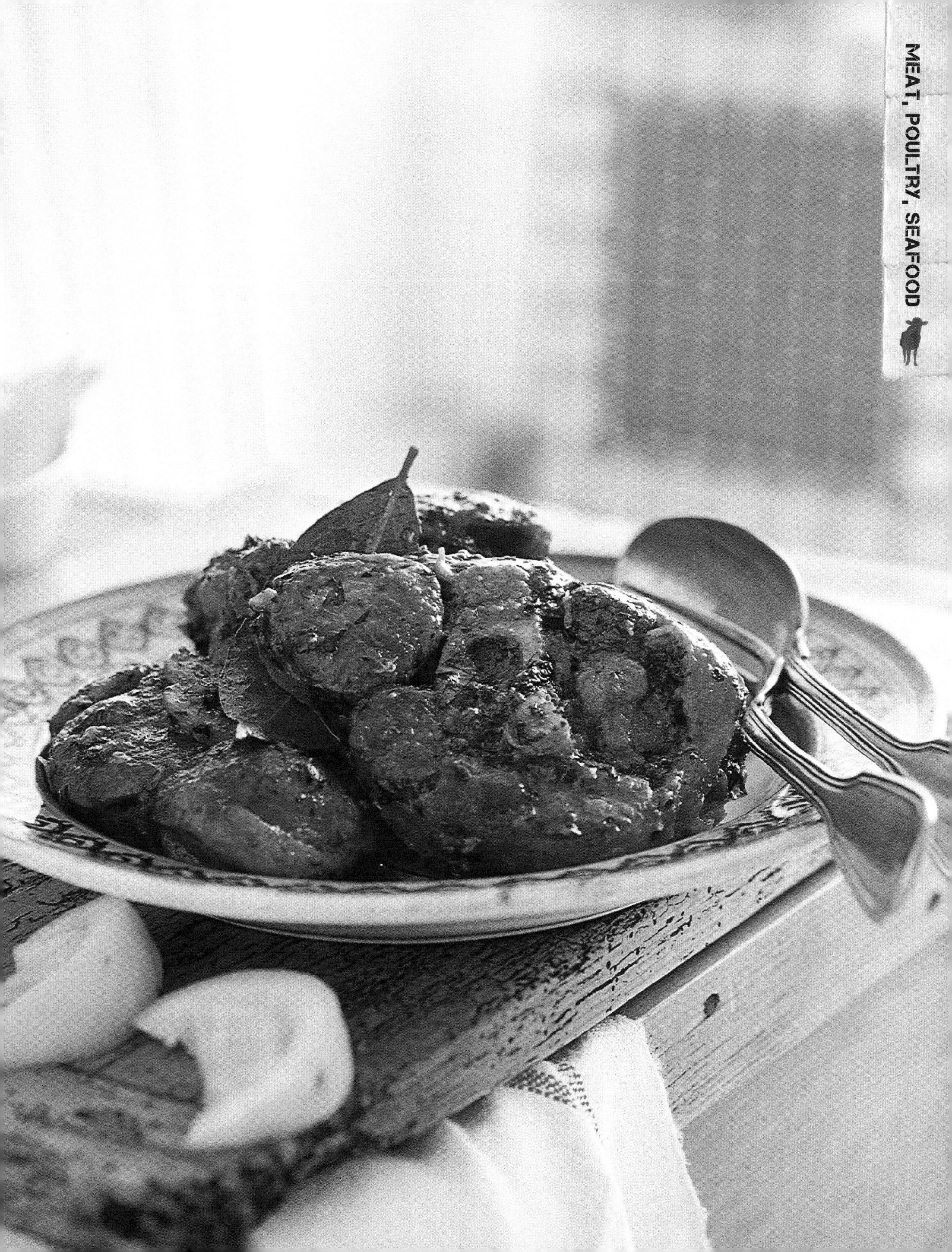

saltimbocca

serves 4

8 small veal escalopes
8 slices of prosciutto
8 sage leaves
2 tablespoons olive oil

60 g (2¼ oz) butter
185 ml (6 fl oz / ¾ cup) dry
    marsala or dry white wine

Place the veal slices between two sheets of plastic wrap and pound using a meat pounder until about 5 mm (¼ inch) thick. Season lightly with sea salt and freshly ground black pepper. Cut the prosciutto slices to the same size as the veal. Cover each piece of veal with a prosciutto slice and place a sage leaf in the centre. Secure the sage leaf with a cocktail stick or toothpick.

Heat the olive oil and half the butter in a large frying pan. Add the veal in batches, prosciutto side up, and fry over medium heat for 3–4 minutes, or until the veal is just cooked through. Turn and fry the prosciutto side, transferring each batch to a warm plate.

Pour off the oil from the pan and add the marsala. Bring to the boil and cook over high heat until reduced by half, stirring to loosen any bits stuck to the bottom of the pan. Add the remaining butter and, when it has melted, season the sauce to taste with sea salt and freshly ground black pepper. Divide the saltimbocca among four warmed plates, remove the cocktail sticks and spoon the sauce over to serve.

parmesan & rosemary-crusted veal chops with salsa rossa

Serves 4

salsa rossa

3 tablespoons olive oil

3 large onions, finely sliced

3 large red capsicums (peppers), cut into 1 cm (½ inch) wide strips

¼ teaspoon chilli flakes

400 g (14 oz) tin chopped tomatoes

4 veal chops, trimmed

150 g (5½ oz/2 cups) fresh white breadcrumbs

75 g (2½ oz/¾ cup) grated parmesan cheese

1 tablespoon finely chopped rosemary

2 eggs

3 tablespoons olive oil

60 g (2¼ oz) butter

4 garlic cloves, bruised

To make the salsa rossa, heat the olive oil in a heavy-based frying pan. Add the onion and cook over medium heat for 5 minutes, or until soft but not browned. Add the capsicum and cook, stirring occasionally, for 30 minutes, or until very soft. Add the chilli flakes and tomatoes and season with sea salt. Simmer for a further 25 minutes, or until the sauce has thickened and the oil has separated from the tomatoes.

Check the seasoning and adjust if necessary. Keep warm.

Meanwhile, using a meat pounder, flatten the veal until 1 cm (1/2 inch) thick. Pat dry with paper towels.

Combine the breadcrumbs, parmesan and rosemary in a shallow bowl. Beat the eggs in a separate bowl and lightly season with sea salt and freshly ground black pepper.

Dip each veal chop in the beaten egg, draining off the excess, then press both sides firmly in the breadcrumb mixture.

Heat the olive oil and butter in a large, heavy-based frying pan over low heat. Add the garlic and cook until golden. Discard the garlic.

Increase the heat to medium, add the veal and cook for 4–5 minutes on each side, or until the crumbs are golden and crisp and the meat is just cooked through. Remove to a warmed plate, cover loosely with foil and leave to rest for 4–5 minutes.

Transfer the veal to four warmed plates, season lightly and serve with the salsa rossa.

beef cooked in ragù

serves 6

This dish is both a starter and main course in one pot. Serve the ragù on spaghetti or bucatini as a first course, and the beef with vegetables or a salad for the main. Ragù is the traditional tomato-based sauce of Bologna.

1 x 1.5 kg (3 lb 5 oz) piece of beef, such as top rump or silverside

60 g (2¼ oz) pork fat, cut into small thin pieces

30 g (1 oz) butter

3 tablespoons olive oil

pinch of cayenne pepper

2 garlic cloves, finely chopped

2 onions, finely chopped

2 carrots, finely chopped

1 celery stalk, finely chopped

½ red capsicum (pepper), finely chopped

3 leeks, sliced

185 ml (¾ cup) red wine

1 tablespoon tomato paste (purée)

375 ml (1½ cups) beef stock

185 ml (¾ cup) tomato passata

8 basil leaves, torn into pieces

½ teaspoon finely chopped oregano leaves, or ¼ teaspoon dried oregano

2 tablespoons finely chopped parsley

60 ml (¼ cup) thick (double/heavy) cream

Make deep incisions all over the beef with the point of a sharp knife, then push a piece of pork fat into each incision.

Heat the butter and olive oil in a large casserole and brown the beef for 10–12 minutes, until it is browned all over. Season with salt and add the cayenne, garlic, onion, carrot, celery, pepper and leek. Cook over moderate heat for 10 minutes until the vegetables are lightly browned.

Increase the heat, add the wine and boil until it has evaporated. Stir in the tomato paste, then add the stock. Simmer for 30 minutes. Add the passata, basil and oregano and season with pepper. Cover the casserole and cook for about 1 hour, or until the beef is tender.

Remove the beef from the casserole and allow to rest for 10 minutes before carving. Taste the sauce for salt and pepper and stir in the parsley and cream.

carpetbag burgers with tarragon mayonnaise

serves 6

tarragon mayonnaise
2 egg yolks, at room temperature

2 teaspoons dijon mustard

1 tablespoon tarragon vinegar, or to taste

200 ml (7 fl oz) olive oil

1 tablespoon finely chopped tarragon

750 g (1 lb 10 oz) minced (ground) beef

80 g (2¾ oz/1 cup) fresh white breadcrumbs

½ teaspoon finely grated lemon zest

5 drops of Tabasco sauce

1 egg, lightly beaten

6 oysters

olive oil, for brushing

6 good-quality hamburger buns finely shredded lettuce, to serve

To make the tarragon mayonnaise, put the egg yolks, mustard and vinegar in a bowl and whisk together well. Whisking constantly, add the olive oil, a little at a time, making sure it is emulsified before adding more oil. Whisk until thick and creamy. Season to taste with sea salt and freshly ground black pepper, adding a little more vinegar if needed, then stir in the tarragon. Cover the surface of the mayonnaise directly with plastic wrap to prevent a skin forming.

To make the burgers, put the beef, breadcrumbs, lemon zest, Tabasco and egg in a large bowl and mix together well. Divide into six equal portions, then shape into patties 1.5 cm (⅝ inch) thick. With your thumb, make a cavity in the top of each burger. Place an oyster in the cavity and smooth the meat over to enclose the oyster completely. Refrigerate until required.

Heat a frying pan and brush lightly with olive oil. Cook the burgers on medium–high heat for 8 minutes on each side, turning only once. Meanwhile, split the hamburger buns and lightly toast them, cut side up, under a hot grill (broiler). Keep warm.

Serve the burgers on the toasted buns with shredded lettuce and the tarragon mayonnaise.

chilli con carne

serves 6

1 tablespoon olive oil

1 brown onion, chopped

3 garlic cloves, crushed

2 tablespoons ground cumin

1½ teaspoons chilli powder

600 g (1 lb 5 oz) minced (ground) beef

400 g (14 oz) tin crushed tomatoes

2 tablespoons tomato paste (concentrated purée)

2 teaspoons dried oregano

1 teaspoon dried thyme

500 ml (17 fl oz/2 cups) beef stock

1 teaspoon sugar

300 g (10½ oz) tin red kidney beans, rinsed and drained

125 g (4½ oz/1 cup) grated cheddar cheese

125 g (4½ oz/½ cup) sour cream

coriander (cilantro) sprigs, to garnish

corn chips, to serve

Heat the oil in a large saucepan over medium heat, add the onion and cook for 5 minutes, or until starting to brown. Add the garlic, cumin, chilli powder and minced beef, and cook, stirring, for 5 minutes, or until the mince has changed colour. Break up any lumps with the back of a wooden spoon. Add the tomato, tomato paste, herbs, beef stock and sugar, and stir to combine. Bring to the boil then reduce to a simmer and cook, stirring occasionally, for 1 hour, or until the sauce is rich and thick. Stir in the beans and cook for 2 minutes to heat through.

Divide the chilli con carne among six serving bowls, sprinkle with the cheese and top each with a tablespoon of the sour cream. Garnish with the coriander sprigs and serve with the corn chips.

SELECTION & STORAGE

The art of hanging, aging and packaging beef

Unless you're in the cattle industry, very few of us know what happens to beef before it reaches the butcher shop or supermarket shelf.

Until about 30 years ago, beef was commonly dry-aged before it was sold. Dry-aging involves hanging beef, either as half-carcasses or large chunks, in a humidity-controlled near-freezing cool room for 10–14 days, or even up to 28 days. During this time, natural enzymes in the meat break down connective tissues and fibres, making the flesh more tender. Significant moisture loss also occurs, resulting in deeper, more concentrated, slightly tangy beef flavours and a denser meat (which also cooks more quickly). Only the best grades of beef are dry-aged as the process is expensive, requiring time and space. Consequently it is no longer a mainstream practice, although if you ask among your local butchers, you may find a caring retailer who still hangs their beef, most likely for high-end restaurateurs.

In the West, most meat is now vacuum-packed within 24 hours of slaughter and sold within 4 days. If the meat is aged at all, it is most likely 'wet-aged' (in vacuum-sealed packs) at a cool temperature for 7–28 days. The same enzymes are still breaking down the same proteins, but because it occurs in a sealed, wet environment, the meat stays very juicy—although it doesn't have the depth of flavour as dry-aged meat and some say it can taste 'bloody' or 'metallic'. With wet-aged meat, take care that there is no excess blood in the packaging, as the meat may develop 'off' flavours.

BUYING AND STORING BEEF

Do buy beef from a specialist butcher. Look for beef that is deep red and slightly moist, with a smooth grain. It should smell sweet and fresh. Visible fat can vary in colour—that of grain-fed cattle tends to be creamy-white, and grass-fed cattle darker. Avoid meat with very yellowish fat as the meat is well past its prime.

Do not buy meat that is very dark purple, brownish, splotchy or very wet, or has a sticky surface or unpleasant smell. Take care not to confuse 'old' meat with 'aged' meat—they are very different things.

Fresh beef can be refrigerated for up to 4 days, but use mince (ground beef) within 2 days. Make sure the beef is dry and not sitting in blood—place larger cuts on a rack above a tray or plate to avoid

Free range, organic, corn-fed?

With so many options, buying chicken is not as straightforward as it used to be.

Many consumers are turning towards birds that have been raised more thoughtfully—and taste far better too. However, the terms 'free range' and 'organic' can be hazy. While 'free range' implies the birds have had free run outdoors and are at liberty to eat from a varied diet, this is not necessarily so. In the United States, 'free range' simply means 'the poultry has been allowed access to the outside'—which could be for as little as 5 minutes per day. In some cases, living conditions are very similar to those of other industrially raised birds. In the United Kingdom, a free-range chicken 'must have daytime access to open-air runs during at least half their life'. In the European Union, 'free range' birds are housed in barns, but must have continuous daylight access to outdoor runs. Also, in most countries, for a bird to be truly 'free range' it must not be subject to routine antibiotic dosing.

Generally, 'organic' poultry is the best option, but do learn about the producer and their practices. With corporations cashing in on the organic bandwagon, be sure you're getting what you think you are paying for.

'Corn fed' chickens have eaten predominantly corn all their lives, and this turns their skin and fat a distinctive yellow colour. The world's most famous corn-fed chicken is the French Poulet de Bresse, so highly regarded that it is protected by its own appellation.

STORING POULTRY

Small young birds such as Cornish game hens or poussin won't keep as long as older birds—use them within one or two days. Fresh chicken, duck and turkey will last for up to four days in the refrigerator if taken from its plastic wrapping. Place it on a plate or in a glass bowl and cover with plastic wrap. Frozen poultry is best used within two months. Always defrost it under refrigeration and ensure it is completely thawed before cooking it. A frozen turkey can take two days to thaw completely in the refrigerator.

this. Store meat in the coldest part of the refrigerator. If it is vacuum packed, leave it in its original wrapping. If it isn't, and you need to refrigerate it for more than a day, remove the plastic and loosely rewrap (so air can flow around it) in fresh plastic wrap or foil. Don't refrigerate larger cuts of meat for longer than 5 days or the meat will turn brown and start to decay.

Vacuum-packed meat will keep, in its original packaging, in the coolest part of the fridge for up to 2 weeks. Store it fat side up to stop it discolouring. When opened, the meat will give off an odour, but this should dissipate after a few minutes. The meat will also change from dark burgundy to bright red upon contact with the air.

Beef can also be frozen for some time; the larger the cut, the longer it will keep. Mince (ground beef)

can be frozen for 2–3 months, and larger pieces for 6 months or even up to 9 months. Make sure it is airtight (to avoid 'freezer burn') and very well wrapped to stop it drying out.

steak au poivre

serves 4

4 x 200 g fillet steaks

2 tablespoons oil

6 tablespoons black peppercorns, crushed

40 g butter

3 tablespoons Cognac

60 ml white wine

125 ml double cream

Rub the steaks on both sides with the oil and press the crushed peppercorns into the meat. Melt the butter in a large frying pan and cook the steaks for 2–4 minutes on each side, depending on how you like your steak.

Add the Cognac and flambé by lighting the pan with your gas flame or a match (stand well back when you do this and keep a pan lid handy for emergencies). Put the steaks on a hot plate. Add the wine to the pan and boil, stirring, for 1 minute to deglaze the pan. Add the cream and stir for 1–2 minutes. Season and pour over the steaks.

baked sticky pork ribs

serves 4

½ small navel orange
125 ml (4 fl oz/½ cup) orange
  juice
1 large garlic clove
½ onion, chopped
1 teaspoon grated fresh ginger
100 ml (3½ fl oz) golden syrup or
  dark corn syrup

1 teaspoon worcestershire sauce
4 drops of Tabasco sauce
2 tablespoons tomato paste
  (concentrated purée)
16 pork spareribs
2 spring onions (scallions), green
  part only, shredded or finely
  sliced on the diagonal

Place the orange in a small saucepan, cover with water and bring to the boil. Reduce the heat and simmer for 5 minutes, or until soft. Drain well, then set aside to cool.

Cut the orange into large chunks, reserving any juice that runs out, then transfer the orange and any reserved juice to a food processor or blender. Add the garlic, onion and ginger and process for 25–30 seconds, or until finely chopped. Add the golden syrup, worcestershire sauce, Tabasco and tomato paste and blend until smooth.

Transfer the marinade to a shallow non-metallic dish, add the pork spareribs and toss to coat well. Cover and refrigerate for 4 hours, turning the ribs occasionally.

Preheat the oven to 180°C (350°F/Gas 4). Place the ribs in a single layer on a large baking tray, pour the marinade over and roast for 20 minutes. Turn the ribs to coat with the sauce, then roast for a further 25–30 minutes, or until tender. Serve hot or at room temperature, sprinkled with the spring onion.

italian meatballs with tomato sauce

serves 4

meatballs

185 ml (6 fl oz/¾ cup) olive oil

1 onion, finely chopped

75 g (2½ oz/½ cup) pine nuts, roughly chopped

3 garlic cloves, crushed

2 large handfuls of parsley, roughly chopped

3 tablespoons roughly chopped basil or rosemary

2 teaspoons fennel seeds, ground

50 g (1¾ oz/⅔ cup) fresh breadcrumbs

250 g (9 oz/1 cup) ricotta cheese

3 tablespoons grated parmesan cheese

grated zest of 1 large lemon

1 egg

500 g (1 lb 2 oz) minced (ground) pork

tomato sauce

800 g (1 lb 12 oz) ripe, firm tomatoes, or 2 x 400 g (14 oz) tins chopped tomatoes

100 ml (3½ fl oz) red wine

Start by making the meatballs. Heat half the olive oil in a frying pan. Add the onion and pine nuts and sauté for 5–6 minutes, or until the onion has softened and the pine nuts are light golden. Add the garlic and cook for a few minutes more, then set aside to cool.

Combine the remaining meatball ingredients in a bowl. Add the cooled onion mixture, season with sea salt and freshly ground black pepper and mix until well combined. Fry a piece of the mixture to check the seasoning, and adjust if necessary. Refrigerate for at least 30 minutes or overnight to allow the flavours to develop.

When you're ready to cook, roll the meatball mixture into walnut-sized balls. Heat the remaining olive oil in a large frying pan.Add the meatballs in batches and cook for 8 minutes, or until golden brown all over, turning them now and then and ensuring there is enough oil to prevent the meatballs sticking to the pan. Remove and set aside while making the sauce.

If using fresh tomatoes, score a cross in the base of each tomato using a small, sharp knife. Plunge the tomatoes into boiling water for 20 seconds, then remove and plunge into iced water to cool. Peel the skin away from the cross and finely chop the flesh.

Put the tomatoes and wine in a large saucepan, season with sea salt and freshly ground black pepper and simmer for 5 minutes. Carefully add the meatballs to the sauce. Reduce the heat to a gentle simmer, then cover and cook for a further 10 minutes. Allow to stand for 10 minutes before serving.

green pea & smoked ham chowder

serves 4

This main-meal soup is filling and wholesome, yet light enough to be served on those early spring days when the weather is warm and peas are at their sweetest. Ham hocks can be salty; remove excess salt by soaking the hock in cold water overnight before making the soup.

2 carrots	1 bay leaf
2 tablespoons oil	2 sprigs thyme
1 leek, white part only, sliced	1 teaspoon black peppercorns
2 onions, diced	2 cups shelled peas
2 cloves garlic	3 sprigs mint, plus 1 small handful
1 celery stalk, diced	leaves
1 smoked ham hock	crusty bread to serve

Cut 1 carrot in half lengthwise. Dice the other carrot. Heat the oil in a large, heavy-based saucepan and add all of the carrot, the leek, onion, garlic, and celery. Cover and cook over low heat for 10 minutes. Add the ham hock, bay leaf, thyme sprigs, peppercorns, and 8 cups water. Slowly bring to a boil, then reduce the heat, cover, and simmer for 1 hour, stirring occasionally.

Add half the peas and the mint sprigs to the pan and cook for another hour or until the ham falls off the bones. Remove the bones, pull off any meat still attached, and return this to the pan. Remove and discard the carrot halves. Add the remaining peas and cook uncovered for 5 minutes or until the peas are tender.

Discard the bay leaf, thyme, and mint sprigs. Check the seasoning. Stir in the mint leaves and remove the soup from the heat. Set aside, partially covered, for 3–4 minutes before serving. Serve with crusty bread.

steamed chicken with ginger and spring onion dressing

serves 4

ginger and spring onion dressing

2 x 2 cm ($^3/_4$ x $^3/_4$ inch) piece of fresh ginger, julienned

125 ml (4 fl oz/$^1/_2$ cup) light soy sauce

2 tablespoons shaoxing rice wine

1 garlic clove, crushed

$^1/_2$ teaspoon sesame oil

1 handful coriander (cilantro) stems, finely chopped

4 spring onions (scallions), thinly sliced on the diagonal

6 kaffir lime leaves, crushed

1 lemon grass stem, cut into thirds and bruised

4 x 4 cm (1$^1/_2$ x 1$^1/_2$ inch) piece of fresh ginger, sliced

10 g (1/4 oz) dried shiitake mushrooms

4 boneless, skinless chicken breasts

700 g (1 lb 9 oz/1 bunch) Chinese broccoli, trimmed and cut into thirds

1 handful coriander (cilantro) leaves, roughly chopped, to garnish

To make the dressing, combine all the dressing ingredients in a bowl and set aside.

Fill a wok one-third full of water, add the kaffir lime leaves, lemon grass, ginger and mushrooms and bring to the boil over high heat. Reduce the heat to a simmer. Line a large bamboo steamer with baking paper and punch with holes. Arrange the chicken fillets on top. Sit the steamer over the wok of simmering stock and steam, covered, for 10 minutes, or until the chicken is cooked. Remove and keep warm. Add the Chinese broccoli to the steamer and steam, covered, for 2–3 minutes, or until just wilted. Remove and keep warm.

Strain the cooking liquid through a sieve, reserving the liquid and the mushrooms only. Remove the stems from the mushrooms and discard. Thinly slice the caps and add them to the dressing with 125 ml (4 fl oz/$^1/_2$ cup) of the reserved liquid. Divide the Chinese broccoli among four serving plates, top with the chicken and spoon the dressing over the top. Garnish with the coriander and serve immediately.

chicken cacciatore

serves 4

Just like the french 'chasseur', 'cacciatore' means 'hunter's style'. The dish is originally from central italy, but like so much italian fare, every region has put its own twist on the recipe. This one, with tomatoes, is probably the most widely travelled.

3 tablespoons olive oil

1 large onion, finely chopped

3 garlic cloves, crushed

1 celery stalk, finely chopped

150 g (5½ oz) pancetta, finely chopped

125 g (4½ oz) button mushrooms, thickly sliced

4 chicken drumsticks

4 chicken thighs

80 ml (⅓ cup) dry vermouth or dry white wine

2 x 400 g (14 oz) tins chopped tomatoes

¼ teaspoon brown sugar

1 sprig of oregano, plus 4–5 sprigs to garnish

1 sprig of rosemary

1 bay leaf

Heat half the oil in a large casserole. Add the onion, garlic and celery and cook, stirring from time to time, over moderately low heat for 6–8 minutes until the onion is golden.

Add the pancetta and mushrooms, increase the heat and cook, stirring occasionally, for 4–5 minutes. Spoon onto a plate and set aside.

Add the remaining olive oil to the casserole and lightly brown the chicken pieces, a few at a time. Season them as they brown. Spoon off any excess fat and return all the pieces to the casserole. Add the vermouth, increase the heat and cook until the liquid has almost evaporated.

Add the tomatoes, sugar, oregano, rosemary, bay leaf and 80 ml (⅓ cup) cold water. Bring to the boil then stir in the reserved pancetta mixture. Cover and leave to simmer for 20 minutes, or until the chicken is tender but not falling off the bone.

If the liquid is too thin, remove the chicken from the casserole, increase the heat and boil until thickened. Discard the sprigs of herbs and taste for salt and pepper. Toss in the additional oregano sprigs and the dish is ready to serve.

chicken & spinach orzo soup

serves 4

1 tablespoon olive oil

1 leek, trimmed and cut into quarters lengthways, then rinsed well and thinly sliced

2 garlic cloves, crushed

1 teaspoon ground cumin

1.5 litres (52 fl oz/6 cups) chicken stock

2 boneless, skinless chicken breasts, about 500 g (1 lb 2 oz) in total

200 g (7 oz/1 cup) orzo

150 g (5½ oz/3 cups) baby English spinach leaves, roughly chopped

1 tablespoon chopped dill

2 teaspoons lemon juice

Heat the olive oil in a large saucepan over low heat. Add the leek and sauté for 8–10 minutes, or until soft. Add the garlic and cumin and cook for 1 minute.

Pour in the stock, increase the heat to high and bring to the boil. Reduce the heat to low, add the chicken breasts, then cover and simmer for 8 minutes. Remove the chicken, reserving the liquid (keep it covered over low heat to keep it hot). When the chicken is cool enough to handle, shred it finely using your fingers. Stir the orzo into the simmering stock and simmer for 12 minutes, or until *al dente*.

Return the chicken to the pan and add the spinach and dill. Simmer for 2 minutes, or until the spinach has wilted. Stir in the lemon juice, season to taste with sea salt and freshly ground black pepper and serve.

chicken with lemon, parsley, pecorino & orecchiette

serves 4

375 g (13 oz) dried orecchiette or other pasta shapes

2 tablespoons extra virgin olive oil

60 g (2¼ oz) butter

4 small boneless, skinless chicken breasts

4 tablespoons lemon juice

2 large handfuls of finely chopped flat-leaf (Italian) parsley

3 tablespoons toasted pine nuts

90 g (3¼ oz/1 cup) grated pecorino cheese

lemon wedges, to serve

Cook the pasta in a saucepan of boiling salted water until *al dente*. Drain and return to the pan to keep warm. Meanwhile, heat the olive oil and half the butter in a large heavy-based frying pan. Add the chicken breasts and cook over medium heat for 2 minutes on each side, then remove from the pan—the chicken will not be quite cooked through.

Add the lemon juice, parsley, pine nuts and remaining butter to the pan. Cook, stirring, for 1–2 minutes, or until the butter has melted and the mixture is well combined. Return the chicken breasts to the pan and cook over low heat for 3–4 minutes, or until the chicken is cooked through, turning once. Season with sea salt and freshly ground black pepper.

Pour the pan juices over the pasta. Add the pecorino to the pasta, toss well, then divide among four warmed bowls. Top each bowl with a chicken breast and serve immediately with lemon wedges.

chargrilled chicken with spinach and raspberries

Serves 4

2 tablespoons raspberry vinegar
2 tablespoons lime juice
2 garlic cloves, crushed
1 tablespoon chopped oregano
1 teaspoon soft brown sugar
2 small red chillies, finely chopped
3 tablespoons extra virgin olive oil
4 boneless, skinless chicken
   breasts

200 g (7 oz/4½ cups) baby
   English spinach leaves
250 g (9 oz) fresh raspberries

dressing

3 tablespoons extra virgin olive oil
1 tablespoon raspberry vinegar
1 tablespoon chopped oregano
1 teaspoon dijon mustard
¼ teaspoon sea salt

In a large bowl, mix together the vinegar, lime juice, garlic, oregano, sugar, chilli and olive oil. Add the chicken breasts, turning to coat, then cover and refrigerate for 2 hours. Preheat the oven to 180°C (350°F/Gas 4).

Heat a chargrill pan or barbecue chargrill plate to medium–high. Cook the chicken for 3 minutes on each side. Place the chicken breasts on a baking tray and bake for 5 minutes, or until just cooked through. Remove from the oven, cover loosely with foil and leave to rest in a warm place for 5 minutes. Carve each breast on the diagonal into five pieces.

Mix together the dressing ingredients and season to taste with freshly ground black pepper. Gently toss the spinach and raspberries in a serving bowl with half the dressing. Arrange the chicken over the top and drizzle with the remaining dressing.

Spanish duck with smoked paprika, pears & toasted almonds

serves 4

for the stock

- 1 tablespoon olive oil
- 1 small carrot, cut into chunks
- 1 onion, cut into chunks
- 2 bay leaves
- 1 thyme sprig
- 1 parsley sprig
- 6 black peppercorns

- 2 kg (4 lb 8 oz) whole duck, cut into 8 pieces
- ¼ teaspoon freshly ground nutmeg
- ½ teaspoon sweet smoked paprika
- a pinch of ground cloves
- 1 tablespoon olive oil
- 8 shallots, peeled
- 8 baby carrots, trimmed
- 2 garlic cloves, cut into slivers
- 4 tablespoons rich cream sherry
- 1 cinnamon stick
- 4 firm ripe pears, cut in half and cored
- 60 g (2¼ oz/heaped ⅓ cup) whole blanched almonds, roasted
- 2½ tablespoons grated dark bittersweet chocolate

Make stock a day ahead using wings and neck of duck. Heat olive oil in a large saucepan, add duck wings, neck, carrot and onion and cook over medium heat, stirring occasionally, for 15–20 minutes, or until browned.

Add 1.25 litres (44 fl oz/5 cups) cold water, the bay leaves, thyme and parsley sprigs and peppercorns. Bring to the boil, then reduce the heat to low. Cover and simmer for 2 hours. Strain stock, discarding solids, then set aside to cool. Refrigerate overnight. The next day, remove the fat. Preheat the oven to 180°C (350°F/Gas 4).

In a small bowl, combine nutmeg, paprika and cloves with a little sea salt and black pepper. Dust duck pieces with spice mixture. Heat the olive oil in a flameproof casserole dish, then brown duck pieces in batches for 6–7 minutes over medium–high heat, turning once. Set the duck aside. Drain off all but 1 teaspoon of fat from the casserole dish. Add shallots and carrots and sauté over medium heat for 3–4 minutes, or until lightly browned. Add garlic and cook for a further 2 minutes. Add sherry and stir well to loosen any bits stuck to the bottom of pan, then add the duck stock, cinnamon stick and all the duck pieces.

Bring to boil, cover with a tight-fitting lid and transfer to oven. Bake for 1 hour 10 minutes, turning duck halfway through. Add pears and bake for a further 20 minutes, or until duck is tender. Meanwhile, process almonds in a food processor until finely ground. Tip into a bowl, add chocolate and stir to combine. Using a slotted spoon, remove duck and pears from stock and transfer to a serving dish with carrots, shallots and cinnamon stick. Cover and keep warm. Bring stock to boil, then cook over high heat for 7–10 minutes, or until reduced by half. Add 3 tablespoons of hot liquid to almond and chocolate mixture, stir well, then whisk into reduced sauce to thicken. Season to taste, pour over the duck and serve.

duck à l'orange

serves 4

This brilliant combination dates back from the 17th Century. The French aren't usually fond of sweet-savoury combinations, so this delicious dish is a little unusual. Roasting the bird on a rack is important here as it allows much of the duck fat to drain off during cooking, resulting in a moist, but not greasy, roast.

5 oranges
2 kg (4 lb 8 oz) whole duck
2 cinnamon sticks
15 g (½ oz) mint leaves
95 g (3¼ oz) light brown sugar

125 ml (4 fl oz/½ cup) cider vinegar
80 ml (2½ fl oz/⅓ cup) Grand Marnier
30 g (1 oz) butter

Preheat the oven to 150°C (300°F/Gas 2). Halve two of the oranges and rub all over the duck. Place them inside the duck cavity with the cinnamon sticks and mint. Tie the legs together and tie the wings together. Prick all over with a fork .Put the duck on a rack, breast side down, and put the rack in a shallow roasting tin. Roast for 45 minutes, turning halfway through.

Meanwhile, zest and juice the remaining oranges Heat the sugar in a saucepan over low heat until it melts and then caramelizes. Swirl the pan gently to make sure it caramelizes evenly. When the sugar is a rich brown, add the vinegar and boil for 3 minutes. Add the orange juice and Grand Marnier and simmer for 2 minutes.

Blanch the orange zest in boiling water for 1 minute three times, changing the water each time. Refresh under cold water, drain and reserve. Remove the excess fat from the tin. Increase the oven temperature to 180°C (350°F/Gas 4). Spoon some of the orange sauce over the duck and roast for 45 minutes, spooning the remaining sauce over the duck every 5 to 10 minutes and turning the duck to baste all sides.

Remove the duck from the oven, cover with foil and strain the juices back into a saucepan. Skim off any excess fat and add the orange zest and butter to the saucepan. Stir to melt the butter. Reheat the sauce and serve over the duck.

fettuccine primavera with smoked salmon

serves 4

In Italy, pasta primavera heralds the arrival of springtime. This variation combines young runner beans, asparagus and snow peas—the best of green spring vegetables—in a light, creamy sauce. Smoked salmon adds a lush richness.

100 g (3½ oz) smoked salmon, sliced

125 g (4½ oz/1¾ cups) baby green beans

12 asparagus spears, trimmed

60 g (2¼ oz/⅔ cup) snow peas (mangetout), ends removed

350 g (12 oz) fettuccine

250 g (9 oz/1 cup) crème fraîche

125 ml (4 fl oz/½ cup) light cream

1 teaspoon lime zest, finely grated

1 small handful basil, torn if large

Cut the smoked salmon into 2 x 5 cm (¾ x 2 inch) strips. Halve the beans diagonally. Cut the asparagus into 4 cm (1½ inch) lengths. Slice the snow peas diagonally. Bring a large saucepan of salted water to a boil. Add the beans, simmer for 2 minutes, and then add the asparagus and simmer for 2 minutes more. Add the snow peas during the last 30 seconds of cooking. Remove all the vegetables from the pan using a slotted spoon.

Return the water to a boil and cook the fettuccine until *al dente*. Meanwhile, combine the crème fraîche and cream in a small saucepan. Season well with salt and freshly ground black pepper and bring to a boil. Simmer for 2 minutes, then reduce the heat to low. Add the lime zest.

Drain the pasta and return it to the pan. Add the cream mixture, salmon, basil and vegetables. Toss to coat and serve immediately.

spaghetti with prawns, clams & scallops

serves 4

250 ml (1 cup) dry white wine
  pinch of saffron threads
1 kg (2 lb 4 oz) clams (vongole)
4 baby octopus
200 g (7 oz) small squid tubes
500 g (1 lb 2 oz) prawns (shrimp)
6 tomatoes

400 g (14 oz) spaghetti
4 tablespoons olive oil
3 garlic cloves, crushed
8–10 scallops, cleaned
6 tablespoons chopped parsley
lemon wedges

Put the wine and saffron in a bowl and leave to infuse. Clean the clams by scrubbing them thoroughly and scraping off any barnacles. Rinse well under running water and discard any that are broken or open and don't close when tapped on the work surface. Place them in a large saucepan with 185 ml (¾ cup) water. Cover the pan and cook over high heat for 1–2 minutes, or until they open (discard any that stay closed after that time). Drain, reserving the liquid. Remove the clams from their shells and set aside.

Clean the octopus by slitting the head and pulling out the innards. Cut out the eyes and hard beak and rinse. Lie the squid out flat, skin side up, and score a crisscross pattern into the flesh, being careful not to cut all the way through. Slice diagonally into 2 x 4 cm (¾ x 1½ inch) strips. Peel and devein the prawns.

Score a cross in the top of each tomato, plunge them into boiling water for 20 seconds, then drain and peel the skin away from the cross. Core and chop. Cook the pasta in a large saucepan of boiling salted water until *al dente.*

Meanwhile, heat the oil in a large frying pan and add the garlic and tomato. Stir over moderate heat for 10–15 seconds, then pour in the saffron-infused wine and the reserved clam liquid. Season and simmer for 8–10 minutes, or until reduced by half. Add the squid, prawns and octopus and cook until the squid turns opaque. Add the scallops, clam meat and parsley and cook until the scallops turn opaque.

Drain the spaghetti and return to the pan. Add two-thirds of the sauce, toss well then transfer to a large serving platter. Spoon the remaining sauce over the top and serve with lemon wedges.

smoked trout gougere

serves 4

75 g (2½ oz) butter
120 g (4¼ oz) plain (all-purpose) flour, sifted twice
¼ teaspoon paprika
3 large eggs, beaten
100 g (3½ oz) Gruyere cheese, grated

400 g (14 oz) smoked trout
100 g (3½ oz) watercress, trimmed
30 g (1 oz) butter
20 g (¾ oz) plain (all-purpose) flour
300 ml (10½ fl oz) milk

Preheat the oven to 200°C (400°F/Gas 6) and put a baking tray on the top shelf to heat up.

Melt the butter with 185 ml (6 fl oz/¾ cup) water in a saucepan, then bring it to a rolling boil. Remove from the heat and sift in all the flour and the paprika. Return to the heat and beat continuously with a wooden spoon to make a smooth shiny paste that comes away from the side of the pan. Cool for a few minutes. Beat in the eggs one at a time, until shiny and smooth. The mixture should drop off the spoon but not be too runny. Stir in two-thirds of the cheese.

Spoon the dough round the edge of a shallow, lightly greased baking dish. Put this in the oven on the hot tray and cook for 45–50 minutes, or until the choux is well risen and browned.

Meanwhile, to make the filling, peel the skin off the trout and lift off the top fillet. Pull out the bone. Break the trout into large flakes. Wash the watercress and put in a large saucepan with just the water clinging to the leaves. Cover the pan and steam the watercress for 2 minutes, or until just wilted. Drain, cool and squeeze with your hands to get rid of the excess liquid. Roughly chop the watercress.

Melt the butter in a saucepan, stir in the flour to make a roux and cook, stirring, for 3 minutes over a very low heat without allowing the roux to brown. Remove from the heat and add the milk gradually, stirring after each addition until smooth. Return to the heat and simmer for 3 minutes. Stir in the smoked trout and watercress and season well.

Spoon the trout filling into the centre of the cooked choux pastry and return to the oven for 10 minutes, then serve immediately.

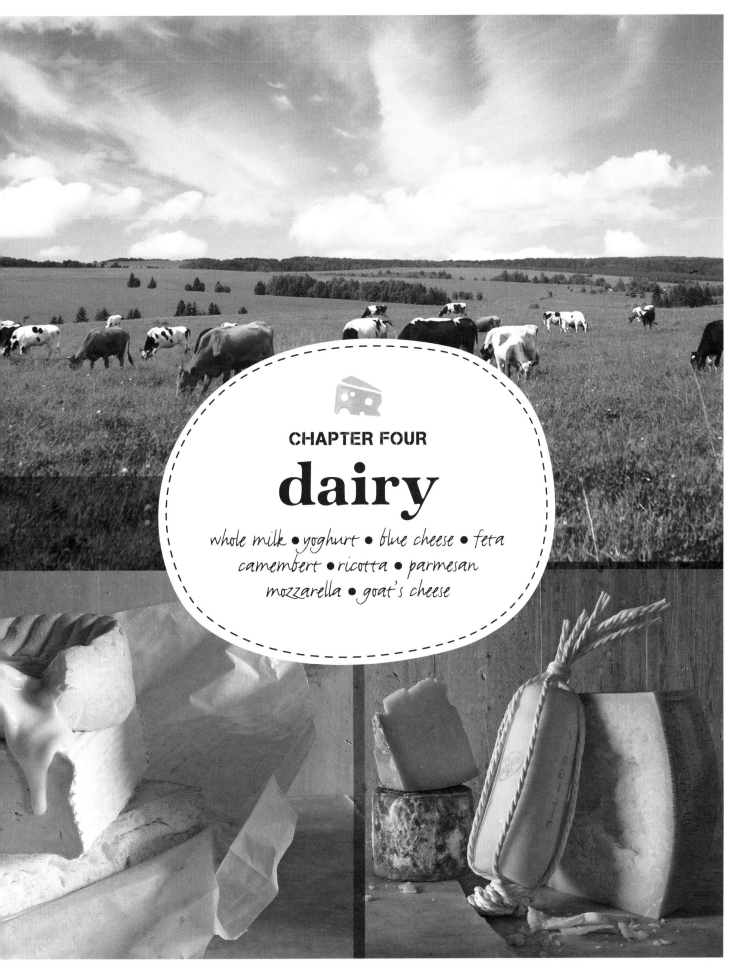

CHAPTER FOUR

dairy

whole milk • yoghurt • blue cheese • feta
camembert • ricotta • parmesan
mozzarella • goat's cheese

baked onions stuffed with goat's cheese & sun-dried tomatoes

serves 6

6 large white onions

60 ml (2 fl oz/$\frac{1}{4}$ cup) extra virgin olive oil

1 garlic clove, crushed

80 g (2$\frac{3}{4}$ oz/$\frac{1}{2}$ cup) sun-dried tomatoes, finely chopped

25 g (1 oz/$\frac{1}{3}$ cup) fresh white breadcrumbs

1 tablespoon chopped parsley

2 teaspoons chopped thyme

100 g (3$\frac{1}{2}$ oz) mild soft goat's cheese, or sheep's milk cheese, crumbled

80 g (2$\frac{3}{4}$ oz/$\frac{3}{4}$ cup) parmesan cheese, grated

1 egg

250 ml (9 fl oz/1 cup) vegetable or chicken stock

1 tablespoon butter

Preheat the oven to 180°C (350°F/ Gas 4). Peel the onions, cut a slice off the top of each and reserve. Using a teaspoon, remove the centre of each onion, almost to the base, to create a cavity. Reserve the onion flesh for another use. Cook the onion shells in a large saucepan of boiling water for 5 minutes, then drain and set aside.

Heat 2 tablespoons of oil in a small frying pan and cook the garlic for 1 minute, or until soft. Add the tomato, breadcrumbs and herbs and cook for 1 minute. Remove from the heat and add the goat's cheese and parmesan. Season to taste, add the egg and stir to combine well.

Divide the mixture among the onion cavities, pushing it in firmly. Place the onions in a large ovenproof ceramic dish. Pour the stock around the onions and drizzle with the remaining oil. Put the onion tops in place, cover the dish with foil and bake for 30 minutes, basting with the cooking juices from time to time. Remove the foil and cook for another 10 minutes.

Transfer the onions to a serving plate, then simmer the remaining stock over medium heat for 5–8 minutes, or until reduced by half and syrupy. Reduce the heat and whisk in the butter. The sauce should be smooth and glossy. Season to taste and spoon over the onions to serve.

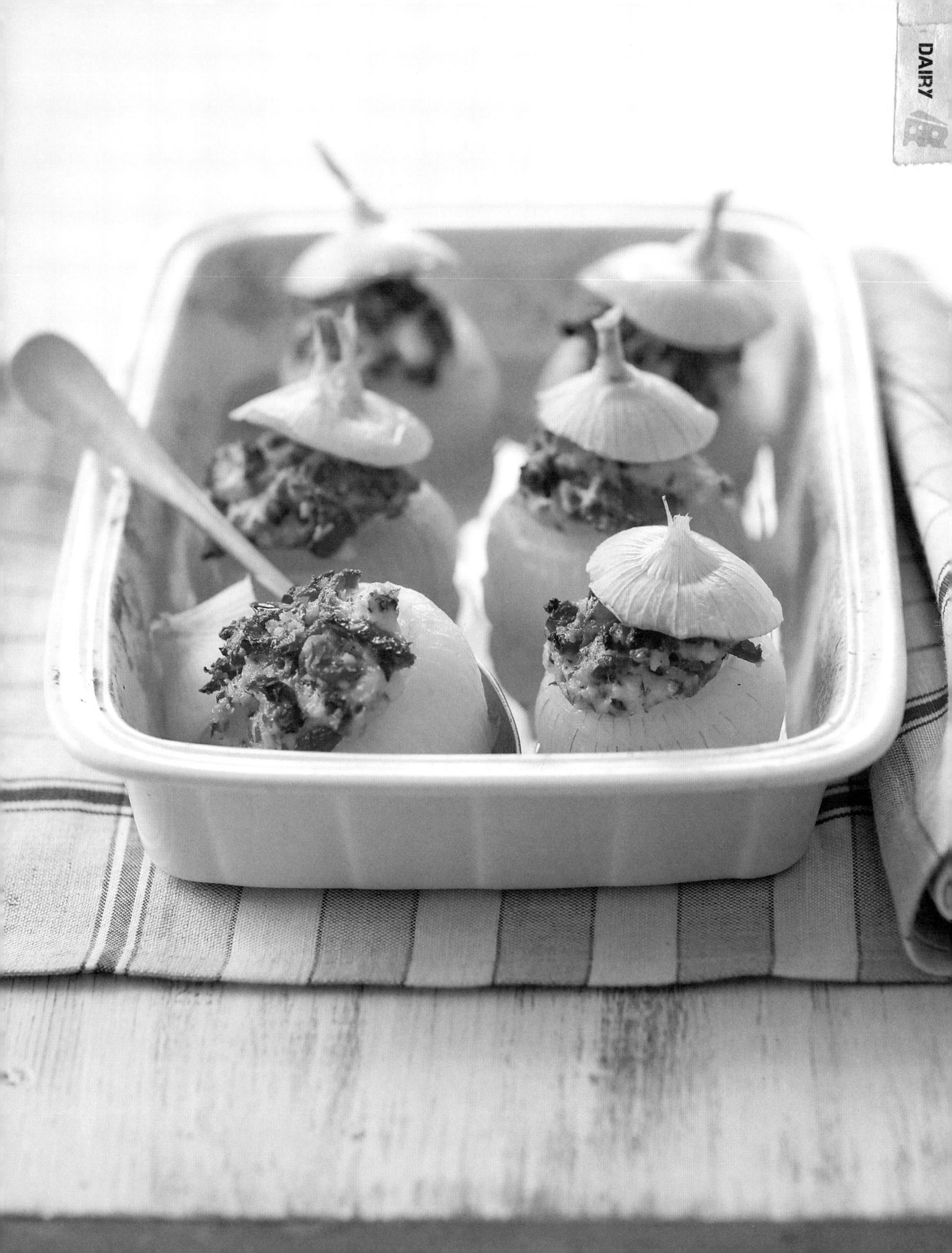

beetroot & blue cheese salad

serves 4

1 tablespoon olive oil

50 g (1¾ oz/½ cup) pecans

1.3 kg (3 lb) small beetroot (beets), washed, trimmed and halved

250 g (9 oz) baby green beans, trimmed

120 g (4¼ oz/4 cups) watercress, trimmed

2 tablespoons walnut oil

1 teaspoon honey

2 teaspoons finely grated orange zest

1 tablespoon cider vinegar

50 g (1¾ oz) firm blue cheese, such as stilton, crumbled

Heat the oil in a frying pan over medium-high heat then add the pecans. Cook, stirring often, for 3 minutes, or until lightly toasted, then sprinkle with salt and freshly ground black pepper. Remove from the heat and pour into a bowl lined with paper towels. Drain.

Line a large steamer with baking paper, punch holes in the paper, place the beetroot in the steamer and cover with a lid. Set the steamer over a saucepan of boiling water and cook the beetroot for 30–35 minutes, or until tender when pierced with a knife. Remove from the steamer and cool, reserving the water in the saucepan.

Remove the baking paper from the steamer, add the beans to the steamer, cover and cook for 5–7 minutes, or until just tender. Remove the beans and refresh under cold water.

Peel the beetroot, trim off any excess stem and cut into wedges or chunks. Combine the pecans, beans and watercress in a large bowl. Whisk together the walnut oil, honey, orange zest and vinegar in a bowl, then pour over the salad. Add the beetroot and stir gently to just combine. Season to taste, then transfer to a serving platter and sprinkle the blue cheese over to serve.

blue cheese soufflé

serves 4

15 g butter, melted
30 g butter
30 g plain flour
250 ml milk

125 g blue cheese, mashed
4 egg yolks
grated nutmeg
5 egg whites

Preheat the oven to 200°C (400°F/Gas 6). Cut a strip of greaseproof paper long enough to fold around a 1.25 litre soufflé dish, then fold in half and tie around the dish so it sticks 2–3 cm above the top. Brush the inside of the dish and the collar with the melted butter and place the dish on a baking tray.

Melt the butter in a heavy-based saucepan and stir in the flour to make a roux. Cook, stirring, for 2 minutes over low heat without allowing the roux to brown. Remove from the heat and add the milk gradually, stirring after each addition until smooth. Return to the heat and bring to the boil. Simmer, stirring, for 3 minutes, then remove from the heat.

Stir the cheese into the sauce until it melts (it might separate but keep stirring—it will correct itself). Beat in the yolks, one at a time, beating well after each addition. Season with nutmeg, salt and pepper and pour into a large mixing bowl.

Whisk the egg whites in a clean dry bowl until they form soft peaks. Spoon a quarter of the egg white onto the soufflé mixture and quickly but lightly fold it in, to loosen the mixture. Lightly fold in the remaining egg white. Pour into the soufflé dish.

Bake for 20–25 minutes, or until the soufflé is well risen and wobbles slightly when tapped. Test with a skewer through a crack in the side of the soufflé—the skewer should come out clean or slightly moist. If the skewer is slightly moist, by the time the soufflé makes it to the table it will be cooked in the centre. Serve immediately.

hot pumpkin with taleggio & herbs

serves 4-6

1 kg (2 lb 4 oz) butternut pumpkin (squash), cut into 4 cm (1½ inch) cubes

125 g (4½ oz) taleggio or other washed-rind cheese, finely sliced

1 tablespoon chopped parsley

1 teaspoon chopped oregano

1 teaspoon thyme

1 teaspoon freshly grated nutmeg

Put the pumpkin in a large steamer and cover with a lid. Sit the steamer over a saucepan or wok of simmering water and steam for 15–20 minutes, or until the pumpkin is nearly tender.

Preheat the oven to 200°C (400°F/Gas 6). Transfer the pumpkin to an ovenproof dish and bake for 30 minutes, or until it is golden brown.

Arrange the cheese on top and bake for a further 3–4 minutes, or until the cheese has melted.

Combine the herbs and nutmeg and sprinkle over the melted cheese. Season well with salt and freshly ground black pepper and serve immediately.

potato, feta & roast garlic pasties

serves 8

400 g (14 oz/3¼ cups) plain (all-purpose) flour

240 g (8½ oz/1 cup) unsalted butter, chilled and cut into cubes

300 g (10½ oz) all-purpose potatoes such as pontiac, unpeeled

8 garlic cloves

2 teaspoons rosemary leaves, chopped

2 tablespoons extra virgin olive oil

80 g (2¾ oz/½ cup) crumbled feta cheese

½ teaspoon grated lemon zest

sea salt

1 egg yolk

1 tablespoon milk

For the pastry, sift the flour and a pinch of salt into a large bowl and add the butter. Using your fingertips, rub in the butter until the mixture resembles coarse breadcrumbs. Make a well in the centre and pour in 120 ml (4 fl oz/½ cup) chilled water. Stir with a flat-bladed knife until a coarse dough begins to form. Transfer to a lightly floured work surface and gently knead until the dough comes together. Shape into a flat disc, wrap in plastic wrap and refrigerate for 30 minutes.

Preheat the oven to 180°C (350°F/Gas 4). Lightly grease a baking tray.

Boil the potatoes in their skins for 15 minutes, or until just cooked. Drain the potatoes, cool, then peel and cut into 1 cm (½ inch) pieces.

Put the garlic, rosemary and 1 tablespoon of the oil onto a piece of foil large enough to enclose them, then twist the edges together to make a secure package. Place on the baking tray and roast for 30 minutes. Cool, then squeeze out the garlic from its skin and roughly chop. Add the garlic to the potato, along with the rosemary and any oil left in the foil package. Add the remaining oil, the feta and lemon zest and gently toss to combine. Season well with freshly ground black pepper and a little sea salt.

Divide the pastry in half. Roll out each half to 3 mm (⅛ inch) thick, then cut into eight 15 cm (6 inch) rounds. Put 2 tablespoons of filling on one half of each pastry round. Combine the egg yolk and milk in a small bowl and lightly brush the unfilled half of the pastry with the egg mix. Fold over the pastry to enclose the filling, pressing gently to seal well. Crimp the edge with your fingers, or gently press with the tines of a fork to seal. Repeat with the remaining filling and pastry rounds.

Place the pasties onto the tray, brush the tops with the remaining egg mixture, then put the tray in the refrigerator for at least 30 minutes. Remove and bake for 30 minutes, or until golden. Allow the pasties to cool a little before serving.

gorgonzola & toasted walnuts on linguine

serves 6

75 g (2½ oz/¾ cup) walnut halves
500 g (1 lb 2 oz) dried linguine
70 g (2½ oz) butter, chopped
150 g (5½ oz) gorgonzola cheese, crumbled

2 tablespoons pouring (whipping) cream
155g (5½ oz/1 cup) shelled fresh peas (approximately 450 g/1 lb in the pod)

Preheat the oven to 180°C (350°F/ Gas 4). Place the walnuts on a baking tray in a single layer and bake for about 5 minutes, or until lightly toasted. Cool.

Cook the linguine in a large saucepan of rapidly boiling salted water until al dente. Drain, then return to the saucepan.

Meanwhile, melt the butter in a small saucepan over low heat and add the gorgonzola, cream and peas. Stir gently for 5 minutes, or until the sauce has thickened. Season to taste. Add the sauce and the walnuts to the pasta and toss until combined well. Serve immediately, sprinkled with freshly ground black pepper.

SELECTION & STORAGE

The art of buying & storing cheese

If you're a cheese lover, you'll know that half the battle is finding a good specialist cheese retailer.

In his *Guide de Fromage*, Pierre Androuët insists that 'a cheesemonger worthy of the name will offer only cheeses that may be eaten within the next 48 hours. For no cheese ... will benefit from being kept too long at home.' While we might not all be fortunate enough to have access to such a cheesemonger, Androuët's statement does underline how important it is to seek out a good, specialist cheese retailer. In general, you won't get great cheese from the supermarket or other mass-market outlets but some wonderful varieties can be found at local farmers' markets or delicatessens. A cheesemonger will offer cheeses cut to order from large wheels or blocks and most often you will be able to taste a little before purchasing. Plastic-wrapped, pre-cut

pieces of cheese suffer from flavour deterioration with prolonged surface exposure to light, air and even to the plastic wrap. A specialist store will keep cheeses at their ideal temperature, which is 12–15ºC (55–60ºF). This is nowhere near as cold as a refrigerator and is more suited to the continuing ripening of cheeses. A cheesemonger will know not to wrap their cheeses tightly, either, as this practice traps moisture and oxygen, promoting bacterial growth. Still-ripening whole cheeses should be kept unwrapped for air circulation, while mature ones should be wrapped in waxed paper. They will carefully tend their cheeses until they are at peak condition; if not, good cheese sellers will know to either not sell the cheese or to sell it with instructions on how to ripen the cheese at home. Cheese is a constantly changing product, and many cheeses go through various ripening stages during which they are perfectly edible—often your own preferences will dictate exactly how ripe or aged you like your cheese. You should only buy as much cheese as you need at a time; that way you won't risk wasting any. Over-ripe cheese will exhibit strong ammoniac or putrid smells.

Assembling a cheese board
A great cheese board can enhance any dinner party – if you do it right.

If you are uncertain where to begin, allow yourself to be guided by a good cheese merchant at your local farmers' market or delicatessen—tell them what you like, explain what will precede the cheese course and follow their advice according to what is in stock and in best condition. It's important to decide whether to serve your cheese course before dessert, as is the French custom, or after it, as do the British. If before, then you can serve wines from dinner with your initial cheese selection(s) then move on to a sweeter dessert wine that is equally suited to stronger cheeses, such as blue cheeses. Soft, mild cheeses are best eaten first and stronger ones last.

You can theme a selection—for example, if you are serving Italian or Spanish food, consider serving cheese from those countries, or those similar in style. Alternatively, you could choose to serve all goat's or sheep's milk cheeses, choosing from a variety of textures, ages and flavours from within those cheese families. Another option is to offer a classic selection that runs the gamut of soft, surface-ripened, hard or semi-hard and blue. It is best to not serve too many types (three to four is sufficient). Or make a feature of just one cheese, such as a wedge of crumbly, aged cheddar, a whole brie or washed rind, or a generous chunk of something blue.

Under no circumstances should you pre-cut or slice the cheeses into small pieces; serve them in the pieces in which they were purchased (unless they are enormous, of course, such as a very large piece of parmesan, and you only want to offer a portion.) Allow 100–150 g (31/2–5 oz) of cheese per guest, perhaps a little more if dinner was light and there is no dessert.

Have your cheeses at room temperature for serving to optimise their flavour; take them out of the fridge at least an hour before serving. If cutting a chunk from a larger piece, do this at the last minute so it doesn't dry out (or, in the case of a whole surface-ripened cheese, so it doesn't ooze out). Place the pieces of cheese on the serving plate with the rind side outermost.

Small knives and plates should be supplied to each person sharing the plate, and accompaniments passed separately.

gnocchi alla Romana

serves 4

750 ml (26 fl oz/4 cups) milk
a pinch of ground nutmeg
200 g (7 oz/1²/₃ cups) fine
  semolina
3 egg yolks
65 g (2¼ oz/²/₃ cup) grated
  parmesan cheese

30 g (1 oz) butter, melted
80 ml (2½ fl oz/⅓ cup) pouring
  (whipping) cream
75 g (2½ oz/½ cup) grated
  mozzarella

Line a deep swiss roll (jelly roll) tin with baking paper. In a saucepan, combine the milk, nutmeg, salt and freshly ground black pepper to taste. Bring to the boil, reduce the heat and gradually stir in the semolina. Cook, stirring frequently, for 5–10 minutes, or until the mixture is very thick.

Remove the pan from the heat and cool slightly. Beat the egg yolks and half the parmesan together in a small bowl. Stir into the semolina, then spread the mixture in the tin. Cool slightly then refrigerate for 1 hour, or until the mixture is firm.

Preheat the oven to 180°C (350°F/Gas 4). Using a floured 4 cm (1½ inch) biscuit (cookie) cutter, cut the semolina into rounds and arrange in a greased shallow overproof dish. Pour the butter and cream over, then sprinkle with the combined mozzarella and remaining parmesan. Bake for 20–25 minutes, or until the gnocchi are golden and bubbling and heated through. Season with freshly ground black pepper and serve.

quiche lorraine

serves 8

220 g (7¾ oz/1½ cups) plain
  (all-purpose) flour
pinch of salt
150 g (5½ oz) unsalted butter,
  chilled and diced
1 egg yolk
25 g (1 oz) butter

300 g (10½ oz) streaky bacon,
  diced
250 ml (9 fl oz/1 cup) thick
  (double/heavy) cream
3 eggs
nutmeg grated

To make the tart pastry, sift the flour and salt into a large bowl, add the butter and rub in with your fingertips until the mixture resembles breadcrumbs. Add the egg yolk and a little cold water (about 2–3 teaspoons) and mix with the blade of a palette knife until the dough just starts to come together. Bring the dough together with your hands and shape into a ball. Wrap in clingfilm and put in the fridge to rest for at least 30 minutes. You can also make the dough in a food processor using the pulse button.

Roll out the pastry into a circle on a lightly floured surface and use to line a tart tin, as directed in the recipe. Trim the edge and pinch up the pastry edge to make an even border raised slightly above the rim of the tin. Slide onto a baking tray and rest in the fridge for 10 minutes.

Preheat the oven to 200°C (400°F/Gas 6). Line a 25 cm (10 inch) fluted loose-based tart tin with the pastry. Line the pastry shell with a crumpled piece of greaseproof paper and baking beads (use dried beans or rice if you don t have beads). Blind bake the pastry for 10 minutes, remove the paper and beads and bake for a further 3–5 minutes, or until the pastry is just cooked but still very pale. Reduce the oven to 180°C (350°F/Gas 4).

Melt the butter in a small frying pan and cook the bacon until golden. Drain on paper towels.

Mix together the cream and eggs and season with salt, pepper and nutmeg. Scatter the bacon into the pastry shell and then pour in the egg mixture. Bake for 30 minutes, or until the filling is set. Leave in the tin for 5 minutes before serving.

roast vegetables with poached egg & camembert

serves 4-6

12 baby onions

2 bunches asparagus, trimmed and
cut into 4 cm (1½ inch) pieces

4 zucchini (courgettes), trimmed
and thickly sliced

2 eggplants (aubergines), cut into
2.5 cm (1 inch) pieces

8 garlic cloves

80 ml (2½ fl oz/⅓ cup) olive oil

2 tablespoons lemon juice

4 eggs

250 g (9 oz) camembert cheese,
cut into 2.5 cm (1 inch) pieces

Preheat the oven to 200°C (400°F/Gas 6). Peel the onions and trim the root
ends, taking care not to cut too much off the root end or the onions will
fall apart.

Combine the onions, asparagus, zucchini, eggplant and garlic in a
roasting dish, drizzle with oil and toss to coat well. Season to taste with
salt and freshly ground black pepper then roast the vegetables for
20 minutes. Drizzle with lemon juice and roast for another 10 minutes.

Bring a large frying pan full of water to the boil, then reduce the heat to
a gentle simmer. Crack an egg into a saucer then gently slip the egg into
the water. Repeat with the remaining eggs, taking care they don't touch
each other, reduce the heat to very low and cook each egg for 3 minutes.

Divide the vegetables among four small ovenproof dishes then arrange
the camembert over the top. Bake for 2–3 minutes, or just until the
cheese begins to melt. Top each dish with a poached egg, season to taste
with freshly ground black pepper and serve immediately.

poached eggs with yoghurt

serves 4

60 g (2¼ oz/¼ cup) butter
1 onion, thinly sliced
250 g (9 oz/1 cup) Greek-style
   yoghurt

4 large eggs
1 teaspoon hot paprika

Preheat the oven to 150°C (300°F/Gas 2). Melt 20 g (¾ oz) of the butter in a heavy-based frying pan, add the onion then cook over low heat, stirring often, for 15 minutes, or until golden. Remove from the pan and cool slightly. Combine the onion and yoghurt in a small bowl then season to taste with salt.

Divide the yoghurt mixture among four deep 7.5 cm (3 inch) diameter ovenproof ramekins then place on a tray in the oven to heat gently.

Meanwhile, fill a large, deep frying pan three-quarters full with water, add a pinch of salt and bring to a gentle simmer. Crack an egg into a saucer, then slide the egg into the simmering water. Poach for 3 minutes, then remove carefully with a slotted spoon and pat off any excess water with paper towels. Poach all the eggs in the same way. Place an egg in each ramekin and season with salt and pepper.

Melt the remaining butter in a small saucepan and add the paprika. Drizzle over the eggs and serve at once.

french onion soup

50 g (1¾ oz) butter
1 tablespoon olive oil
1 kg (2 lb 4 oz) onions, thinly sliced
   into rings
3 x 425 g (15 oz) tins chicken or
   beef consommé

125 ml (4 fl oz/½ cup) dry sherry
half a baguette
125g (4½ oz/1 cup) finely grated
   cheddar or gruyère cheese

Heat the butter and oil in a large saucepan, add the onion and cook, stirring frequently, over low heat for 45 minutes, or until softened and translucent. It is important not to rush this stage—cook the onion thoroughly so that it caramelises and the flavour develops.

Add the consommé, sherry and 1 cup (9 fl oz/250 ml) water. Bring to the boil then reduce the heat and simmer for 30 minutes. Season to taste.

Meanwhile, slice the bread into four thick slices and arrange them in a single layer under a hot grill. Toast one side, remove from the grill, turn over and cover the untoasted side with the gruyere.

Ladle the hot soup into four serving bowls, top each with a slice of toast, cheese side up, and place under the grill until the cheese is melted and golden.

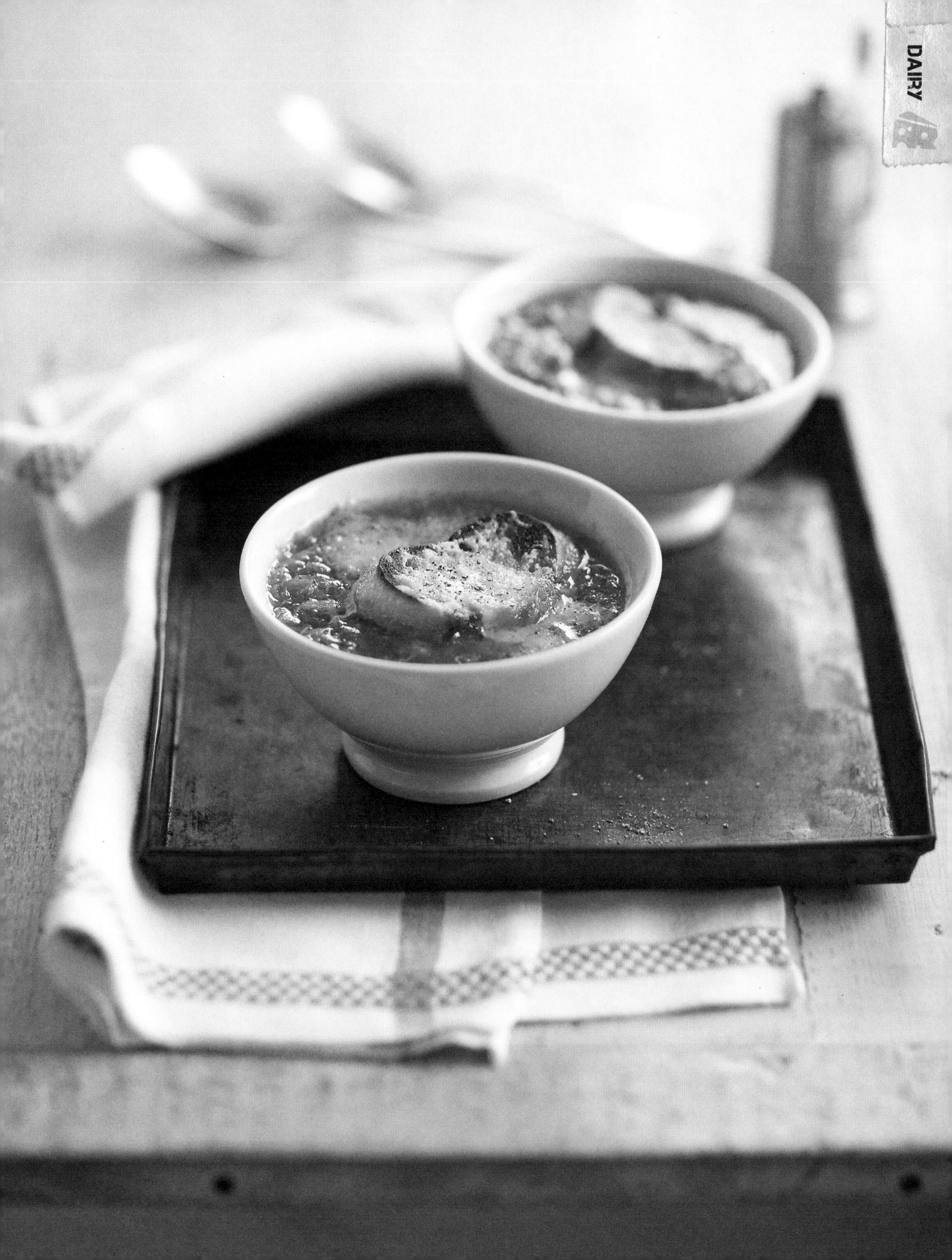

borlotti bean moussaka

Serves 6

250 g (9 oz/1¼ cups) dried
  borlotti beans

2 large eggplants (aubergines)

80 ml (2½ fl oz/⅓ cup) olive oil

1 onion, chopped

1 garlic clove, crushed

125 g (4½ oz) button mushrooms,
  wiped clean and sliced

250 ml (9 fl oz/1 cup) red wine

2 x 440 g (15½ oz) tins diced,
  peeled tomatoes

1 tablespoon tomato paste
  (concentrated purée)

1 tablespoon chopped oregano

topping

250 g (9 oz/1 cup) plain yoghurt

4 eggs, lightly beaten

500 ml (17 fl oz/2 cups) milk

¼ teaspoon sweet paprika

50 g (1¾ oz/½ cup) grated
  parmesan cheese

40 g (1½ oz/½ cup) fresh
  breadcrumbs

Soak the borlotti beans in cold water overnight. Drain well and rinse. Transfer the beans to a saucepan, cover with cold water and bring to the boil. Reduce the heat to a simmer and cook the beans over low heat for 1½ hours, or until tender. Drain well.

Meanwhile, preheat the oven grill (broiler) to medium-high. Slice the eggplant, sprinkle with salt and allow to stand for 30 minutes.

Rinse the eggplant then pat dry on paper towels. Brush the eggplant all over with oil, then grill for 3 minutes on each side, or until golden. Drain the eggplant on paper towels.

Preheat the oven to 200°C (400°F/Gas 6). Heat the remaining oil in a large, heavy-based saucepan. Add the onion and garlic and cook over medium heat for 4–5 minutes, or until the onion is golden. Add the mushrooms and cook for 3 minutes, or until lightly browned. Add the wine and cook over high heat for 2–3 minutes. Stir in the tomatoes, tomato paste and oregano. Bring the mixture to the boil then reduce the heat and simmer for 40 minutes, or until the mixture has reduced and thickened.

Spoon the borlotti beans into a large ovenproof dish and top with the tomato sauce and eggplant slices.

To make the topping, whisk together the yoghurt, eggs, milk and paprika, then pour over the mixture in the dish. Allow to stand for 10 minutes. Combine the parmesan and breadcrumbs in a small bowl then sprinkle over the moussaka. Bake the moussaka for 50–55 minutes, or until hot, bubbling and golden on top.

New York cheesecake

Serves 8-10

pastry

60 g (4 oz/$\frac{1}{2}$ cup) self-raising
flour

230 g (8 oz/$1\frac{3}{4}$ cups) plain
(all-purpose) flour

60 g ($2\frac{1}{4}$ oz/$\frac{1}{4}$ cup) caster
(superfine) sugar

1 teaspoon finely grated lemon
zest

80 g ($2\frac{3}{4}$ oz) butter

2 eggs, lightly beaten

filling

750 g (1 lb 10 oz/3 cups) curd
cheese or cream cheese,
softened

230 g (8 oz/1 cup) caster
(superfine) sugar

60 g ($2\frac{1}{4}$ oz/$\frac{1}{2}$ cup) plain
(all-purpose) flour

2 teaspoons grated orange zest

2 teaspoons grated lemon zest

4 eggs

170 ml ($5\frac{1}{2}$ fl oz/$\frac{2}{3}$ cup) pouring
(whipping) cream

glacé (candied) citrus slices, to
decorate (optional)

Combine the flours, sugar and lemon zest in a bowl, add the butter then, using your fingertips, rub in until the mixture resembles coarse breadcrumbs. Add the egg and mix well. Gradually add 3–4 tablespoons of cold water, or enough to give a coarse dough, then turn out onto a lightly floured surface and gather into a ball. Wrap in plastic wrap and refrigerate for 20 minutes, or until firm.

Preheat the oven to 210°C (415°F/Gas 6–7). Roll the pastry between two sheets of baking paper until large enough to fit the base and side of a greased 22 cm (8 inch) round springform cake tin. Ease the pastry into the tin and trim the edges. Line the pastry shell with a piece of greaseproof paper and baking beads (use dried beans or rice if you don't have beads). Bake the pastry for 10 minutes. Remove the paper and beads and bake for a further 5 minutes, or until the pastry is light golden. Cool.

Reduce the oven to 150°C (300°F/Gas 2). To make the filling, use electric beaters to beat the cream cheese, sugar, flour and zests until smooth. Add the eggs, one at a time, beating well after each addition. Stir in the cream, then pour the filling over the pastry and bake for 1 hour 25 minutes, or until almost set. Cool in the oven, then refrigerate until firm. Serve decorated with glacé citrus slices, if desired.

lime & ricotta pudding

serves 4

This refreshing pudding couldn't be easier to make. Apart from the lime and fresh ricotta, you may already have all the ingredients to hand. The quality of the ricotta is important—it should be crumbly, moist and fresh-tasting, not bland and dull.

60 g (2¼ oz) unsalted butter, softened

350 g (12 oz/1½ cups) caster (superfine) sugar

2 teaspoons lime zest, finely grated

3 eggs, at room temperature, separated

375g (13 oz/1½ cups) fresh ricotta cheese or good-quality tub of ricotta

30 g (1 oz/¼ cup) self-raising flour

60 ml (2 fl oz/¼ cup) lime juice

2 teaspoons icing (confectioners') sugar

Preheat the oven to 180°C (350°F/Gas 4) and grease a 1.5 litre (52 fl oz/6 cup) capacity ovenproof dish.

Using electric beaters, beat the butter and caster sugar with half the lime zest for 30 seconds, or until combined. Add the egg yolks, one at a time, and beat until well combined. Gradually add the ricotta and flour alternately and beat until the mixture is thick and smooth. Stir in the lime juice.

Beat the egg whites until stiff peaks form and gently fold into the ricotta mixture in two batches. Pour the mixture into the prepared dish and place in a roasting tin. Pour enough hot water into the tin to come halfway up the sides of the dish. Bake for 1 hour.

Sift the icing sugar over the warm pudding and sprinkle with the remaining lime zest. Serve warm.

petits pots de crème

serves 4

1 vanilla bean
400 ml (14 fl oz) milk
3 egg yolks

1 egg, lightly beaten
80 g (2¾ oz/⅓ cup) caster
   (superfine) sugar

Preheat the oven to 140°C (275°F/Gas 1). Split the vanilla bean lengthways, scrape out the seeds then combine the bean and seeds with the milk in a saucepan. Bring the milk just to the boil.

Meanwhile, whisk together the egg yolks, egg and sugar in a bowl until well combined. Strain the milk over the egg mixture and stir to combine. Skim the surface to remove any foam.

Ladle the mixture into four 125 ml (4 fl oz/½ cup) ramekins and place in a roasting tin. Pour enough hot water into the tin to come halfway up the sides of the ramekins. Bake for 30 minutes, or until the custards are just firm to the touch. Transfer the ramekins to a wire rack to cool, then refrigerate until ready to serve.

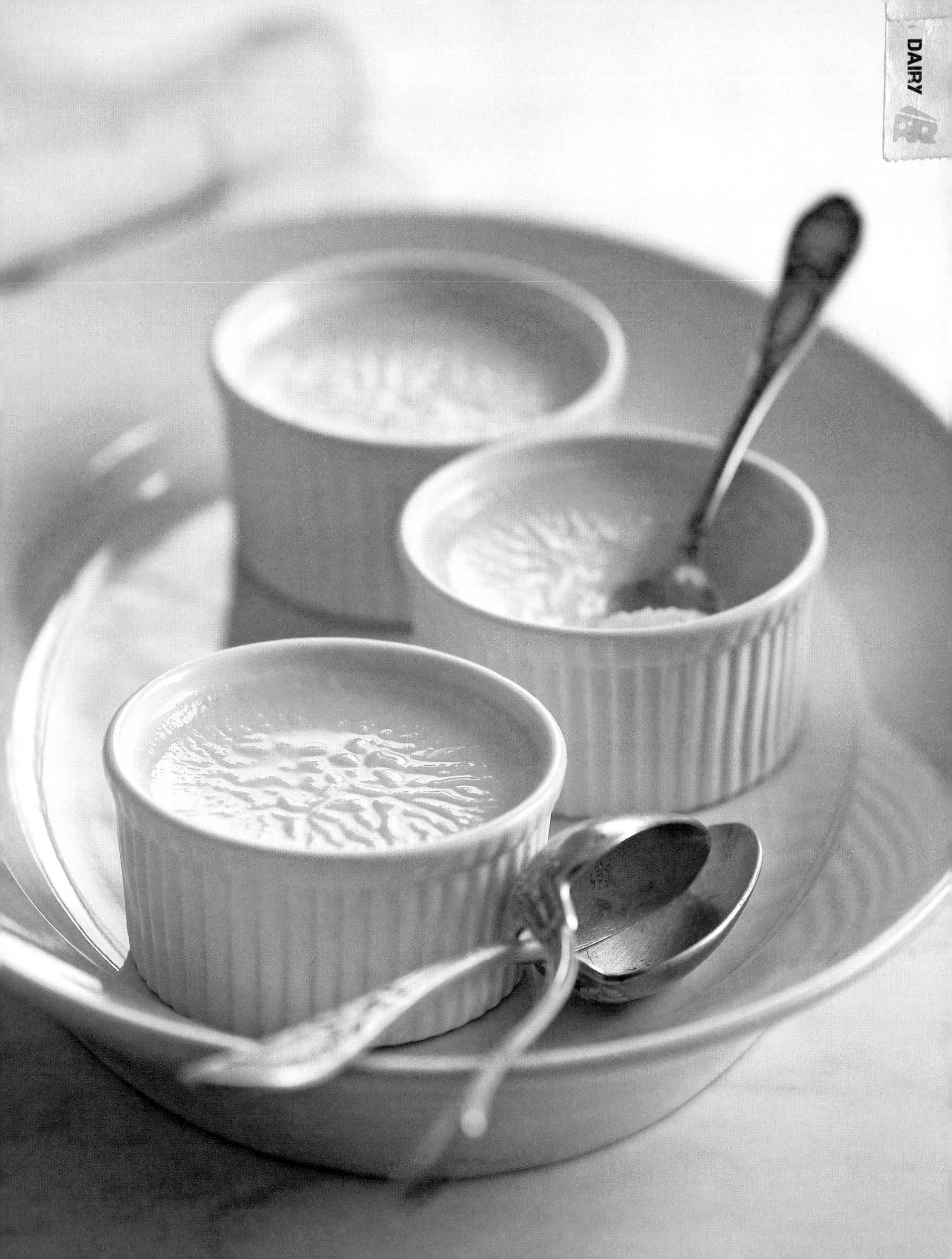

honey parfait with caramelized cumquats

serves 6

90 g (3¼ oz/¼ cup) honey
4 egg yolk, at room temperature
300 ml (10½ fl oz) cream
  (whipping), whipped to soft
  peaks

1 tablespoon orange liqueur, such
  as Grand Marnier
500 g (1 lb 2 oz) cumquats
350 g (12 oz/1½ cups) caster
  (superfine) sugar

Put the honey in a small saucepan and bring to the boil. Beat the egg yolks in a bowl until thick and pale, then add the honey in a slow stream, beating constantly. Gently fold in the cream and liqueur. Pour the mixture into 6 x 125 ml (4 fl oz/½ cup) freezer-proof moulds. Freeze for 4 hours, or until firm.

Wash the cumquats and prick the skins with a skewer. Place the cumquats in a large saucepan, cover with boiling water and simmer for 20 minutes. Strain the cumquats and reserve 500 ml (17 fl oz/2 cups) of the liquid. Return the liquid to the saucepan, add the sugar and stir over medium heat until the sugar has dissolved. Increase the heat and boil for 10 minutes. Add the cumquats and simmer for 20 minutes, or until the cumquats are soft and the skins are smooth and shiny. Remove from the heat and set aside to cool. Lift the cumquats out of the syrup, reserving the syrup.

To serve, dip the moulds in hot water for 5–10 seconds before inverting the parfait onto serving plates. Serve with the caramelized cumquats and a little of the syrup spooned over the top.

chocolate mousse

serves 4-6

300 g dark chocolate, chopped
30 g unsalted butter
2 eggs, lightly beaten
3 tablespoons Cognac

4 egg whites
5 tablespoons caster sugar
500 ml whipping cream

Put the chocolate in a heatproof bowl over a saucepan of simmering water, making sure the base of the bowl isn't touching the water. Leave the chocolate until it looks soft and then stir until melted. Add the butter and stir until melted. Remove the bowl from the saucepan and cool for a few minutes. Add the eggs and Cognac and stir.

Using an electric mixer or balloon whisk, beat the egg whites in a clean dry bowl until soft peaks form, adding the sugar gradually. Whisk one third of the egg white into the chocolate mixture to loosen it and then fold in the remainder with a large metal spoon or spatula.

Whip the cream and fold into the mousse. Pour into glasses or a large bowl, cover and refrigerate for at least 4 hours.

caramel squares

makes 15 squares

185 g (6½ oz/1½ cups) plain
   (all-purpose) flour
1½ tablespoons caster (superfine)
   sugar
100 g (3½ oz) butter, chopped
1 egg

caramel
400 g (14 oz) tin sweetened
   condensed milk
20 g (¾ oz) butter
1 tablespoon golden syrup, dark
   corn syrup or treacle

chocolate topping
120 g (4¼ oz) dark chocolate,
   chopped
40 g (1½ oz) butter

Brush a 17 x 26 cm (6½ x 10½ inch) shallow rectangular tin with melted butter and line the base with baking paper.

Combine the flour and sugar in a bowl, add the butter then, using your fingertips, rub the butter in until the mixture resembles breadcrumbs. Stir in the egg and enough water to form a coarse dough, then press the dough together on a lightly floured surface. Wrap the dough in plastic wrap and refrigerate for 30 minutes, or until firm.

Preheat the oven to 210ºC (415ºF/Gas 6–7). Roll out the pastry between two pieces of baking paper to fit the base of the tin. Cover the pastry in the tin with baking paper, fill with baking beads, dried beans or rice then bake for 10 minutes. Remove the beads and paper then bake for another 10 minutes or until golden. Remove from the oven.

Reduce the oven to 180ºC (350ºF/Gas 4).

To make the caramel, combine all the ingredients in a small saucepan then stir constantly over medium-low heat until the butter melts and the mixture boils and thickens. Spread the caramel in a thin even layer over the pastry and bake for 10 minutes, or until firm. Allow to cool.

To make the topping, combine the chocolate and butter in a bowl set over a saucepan of simmering water. Stir the mixture until melted and well combined, allow to cool slightly then pour over the caramel. Leave to set, then cut into squares.

The squares will keep, stored in an airtight container in a cool, dark place, for 2 days.

CHAPTER FIVE

nuts & spices

hazelnuts • pistachios • pine nuts
cardamom • ginger • turmeric
saffron • star anise

hazelnut & chocolate cake

serves 8

140 g (1 cup) skinned hazelnuts
3 tablespoons cocoa powder
60 g (½ cup) plain (all-purpose) flour
30 g (¼ cup) self-raising flour

185 g (1 cup) soft brown sugar
250 g (9 oz) unsalted butter, softened
4 eggs, separated
icing (confectioners') sugar

Toast the hazelnuts under a hot grill (broiler), turning them so they brown on all sides. Leave them to cool, then put in a food processor and process until fine (don't overprocess or they will become oily), or chop finely with a knife. Transfer to a bowl with the cocoa powder and sifted flours. Preheat the oven to 180°C (350°F/Gas 4).

Beat together the sugar and butter until very creamy. Add the egg yolks one at a time, mixing well after each addition. Add the hazelnut mixture and stir well. Whisk the egg whites in a clean dry glass bowl until stiff peaks form, then fold into the mixture. Pour into the tin and bake for 50 minutes or until a skewer inserted into the centre comes out clean. Rest for 15 minutes, then cool on a wire rack. Dust with icing sugar before serving.

peanut toffee shortbreads

makes 18

110g (3¾ oz) unsalted butter, softened

115g (4oz/½ cup) caster (superfine) sugar

1 egg

185g (6½ oz/ 1½ cups) plain (all-purpose) flour

60g (2¼ oz/½ cup) self-raising flour

180g (6oz) unsalted butter

185g (6½ oz/1 cup) soft brown sugar

2 tablespoons golden syrup or dark corn syrup

½ teaspoon lemon juice

400g (14oz/2½ cups) roasted unsalted peanuts

Preheat the oven to 180C (350F/Gas 4). Lightly grease an 18x27cm (7x10 ¾ inch) baking tin and line the base and sides with baking paper, leaving the paper hanging over the two long sides.

Using electric beaters, cream the butter and sugar until light and fluffy. Add the egg and beat well. Sift the flours into a bowl, then fold into the butter mixture using a large metal spoon until just combined. Press the mixture into the prepared tin.

Bake for 15 minutes, or until the shortbread is firm and lightly coloured. Remove from the oven and leave to cool in the tin for 10 minutes.

To make the topping, put the butter, sugar, golden syrup and lemon juice in a saucepan. Stir over low heat until the sugar has dissolved, then simmer, stirring now and then, for 5 minutes. Stir in the peanuts and remove from the heat.

Spread the topping over the shortbread base using two spoons, taking care as the mixture will be very hot.

Bake for a further 5 minutes. Remove from the oven and leave to cool in the tin for 15 minutes, then turn out onto a board and cut into fingers using a large knife.

Peanut toffee shortbreads will keep for up to 1 week stored in a cool place in an airtight container, or can be frozen in an airtight container for up to 1 month.

date & walnut rolls

makes 2 rolls *(each yields about 8 slices)*

90 g (3¼ oz/¾ cup) self-raising flour

90 g (3¼ oz/¾ cup) plain (all-purpose) flour

½ teaspoon bicarbonate of soda (baking soda)

1 teaspoon mixed (pumpkin pie) spice

125 g (4½ oz/1 cup) chopped walnuts

100 g (3½ oz) unsalted butter, chopped

140 g (5 oz/¾ cup) soft brown sugar

250 g (9 oz/1½ cups) chopped pitted dates

1 egg, lightly beaten

butter, to serve (optional)

Preheat the oven to 180°C (350°F/Gas 4). Lightly grease two 17 x 8 cm (6 ½ x 3¼ inch) nut loaf tins and their lids. Sift the flours, bicarbonate of soda and mixed spice into a large bowl, then stir in the walnuts. Make a well in the centre.

Put the butter, sugar, dates and 125 ml (4 fl oz/½ cup) water in a small saucepan. Stir constantly over low heat until the butter has melted and the sugar has dissolved. Remove from the heat, allow to cool slightly, then add to the well in the flour mixture, along with the egg. Mix well using a wooden spoon.

Spoon the mixture evenly into the prepared tins and set them upright on a baking tray. Bake for 1 hour, or until a cake tester inserted into the centre of the rolls comes out clean. Leave the rolls in the tins with the lids on for 10 minutes, before turning out onto a wire rack to cool.

Cut into slices and serve with butter, if desired. Date and walnut rolls will keep for up to 5 days stored in a cool place in an airtight container, or can be frozen in an airtight container for up to 6 weeks.

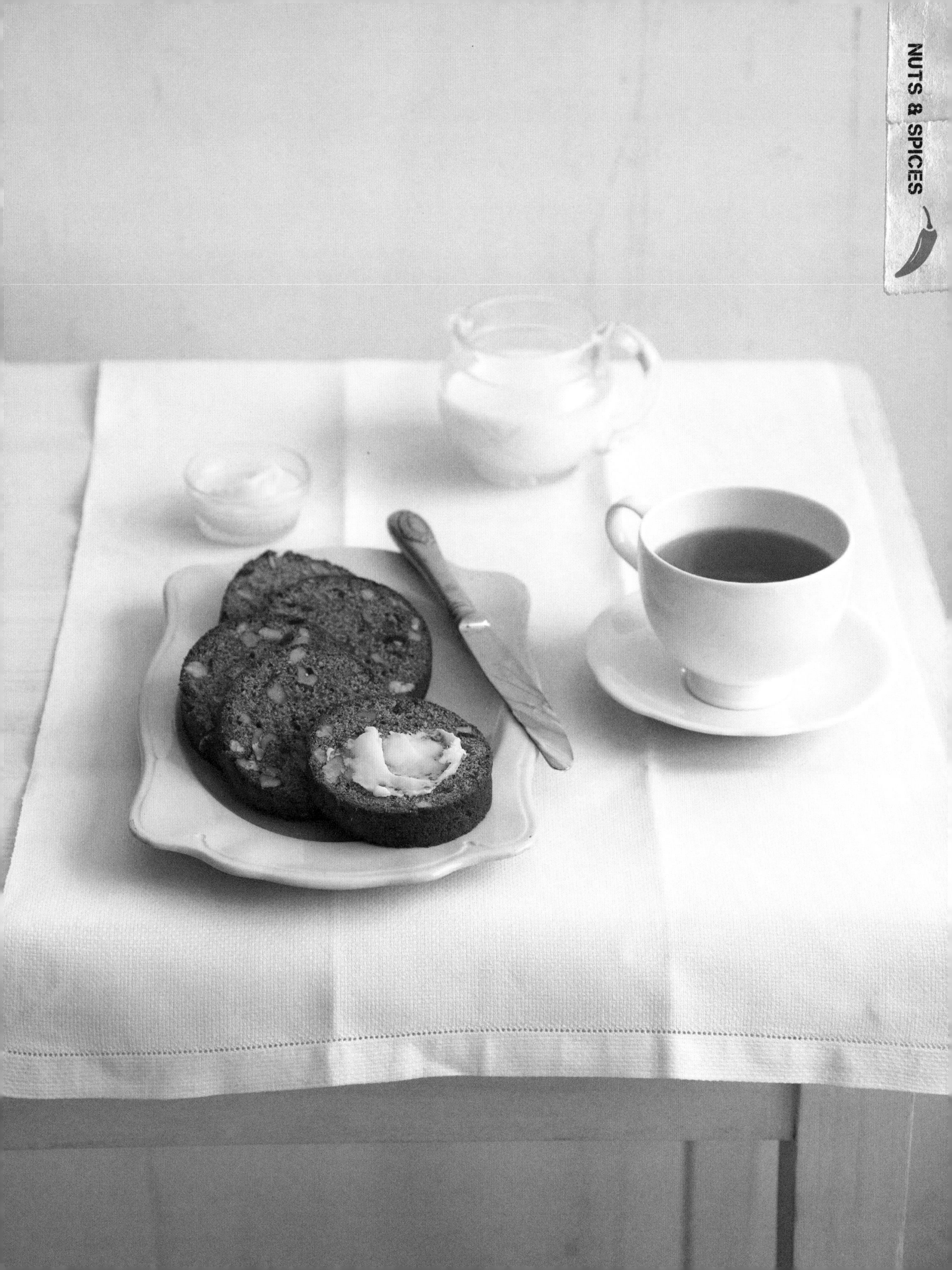

biscotti

makes about 40

375 g (13 oz/3 cups) plain
  (all-purpose) flour
170 g (6 oz/¾ cup) caster
  (superfine) sugar
3 eggs, lightly beaten
½ teaspoon baking powder

½ teaspoon natural vanilla extract
75 g (2½ oz/½ cup) blanched
  almonds
75 g (2½ oz/½ cup) pistachio nuts

Preheat the oven to 180°C (350°F/Gas 4). Line two baking trays with baking paper.

Sift the flour into a large bowl. Add the sugar, eggs, baking powder, vanilla and a pinch of salt. Using a wooden spoon at first and then your hands, mix until a firm, smooth dough forms. Turn out onto a lightly floured work surface and divide the dough in half. Knead the almonds into one portion, and the pistachios into the other.

Roll each portion into a log about 20 cm (8 inches) long. Place one on each baking tray and press down gently to flatten the logs slightly. Bake for 25 minutes, or until lightly golden, then remove from the oven and allow to cool slightly. Reduce the oven temperature to 170°C (325°F/Gas 3).

Using a large, serrated knife, cut each log on the diagonal into slices 1 cm (½ inch) thick, then place back on the baking trays. Bake for a further 15 minutes, or until the biscotti start to brown and are dry to the touch. Remove from the oven and transfer to wire racks to cool.

Biscotti will keep for up to 3 weeks stored in a cool place in an airtight container, or can be frozen in an airtight container for up to 3 months.

SELECTION & STORAGE

walnuts

Buy walnuts with undamaged shells and shake them first—if any rattle, it means the meat has withered inside the shell. The shells protect the meat from insects and light and the nuts will keep, unshelled, for up to 1 year stored in a cool, dark place. Shelled nuts should be refrigerated for up to 3 months or frozen for up to 6 months.

hazelnuts

Purchase hazelnuts that feel full and heavy in their shells. The nuts inside should be plump and the fine brown skin that covers them should be tight. Hazelnuts, like all nuts, are highly perishable so store them away from heat and humidity—in the refrigerator is ideal.

pistachios

Some processors open their pistachios mechanically, so make sure any nuts you buy have been allowed to open naturally on the tree, as their flavour will be superior. Once the pistachios' shell has split, they have a limited shelf life, so store them carefully. This is best done in a container in the refrigerator (for up to 3 months) or frozen, for up to 6 months.

Good pistachios should taste delicately sweet and buttery and be quite green—their characteristic pigment comes from chlorophyll and the greener the pistachios are the better the flavour. The brownish skin which covers the kernels is perfectly edible but can be removed by blanching in boiling water, if desired.

macadamias

The macadamia has the hardest shell of all commercially grown nuts and indicates its ripeness by falling to the ground after the green husk that surrounds it has split. It is then collected, dried and shelled. Because of their very high oil content (up to 80 per cent), macadamias can quickly turn rancid, so store them in an airtight container in the refrigerator for up to 6 months, or in the freezer for up to 1 year.

peanuts

Like all nuts, peanuts contain a high ratio of oil and are prone to rancidity so need to be stored carefully. Buy them in their shells (look closely for any sign of mould as this is common in peanuts) and store them in a well-aerated bag (not in plastic or they could turn mouldy).

almonds

If purchased in their shells, almonds will keep for up to 1 year stored in a cool dark place. Shelled nuts, as prone to rancidity as all other nut types, should be stored in an airtight container in the refrigerator for several months or in the freezer for up to a year. Avoid any that show signs of mould, cracking or holes in their shells—if purchasing shelled almonds, look for ones that are plump and unwrinkled.

glacé fruit & nut cake

serves 20

50 g (1¾ oz) unsalted butter, softened

60 g (2¼ oz/⅓ cup) soft brown sugar

2 eggs

125 g (4½ oz/1 cup) plain (all-purpose) flour

1 teaspoon baking powder

1 teaspoon ground nutmeg

2 tablespoons marmalade

200 g (7 oz/1¼ cups) chopped pitted dates

185 g (6½ oz/1½ cups) raisins

155 g (5½ oz/1 cup) brazil nuts

140 g (5 oz/⅔ cup) red, yellow and green glacé cherries

110 g (3½ oz/½ cup) chopped glacé pear or pineapple

120 g (4¼ oz/½ cup) chopped glacé apricots

120 g (4¼ oz/½ cup) chopped glacé peaches

120 g (4¼ oz/½ cup) chopped glacé figs

100 g (3½ oz/1 cup) walnut halves

100 g (3½ oz/⅔ cup) blanched almonds

topping

2 tablespoons marmalade

2 teaspoons powdered gelatine

150 g (5½ oz/⅔ cup) glacé pear or pineapple rings

100 g (3½ oz/½ cup) red, yellow and green glacé cherries

40 g (1½ oz/¼ cup) blanched almonds

Preheat the oven to 150°C (300°F/Gas 2). Lightly grease and line the base and sides of a 20 x 8 x 7 cm (8 x 3¼ x 2¾ inch) loaf (bar) tin with baking paper.

Using electric beaters, cream the butter and sugar in a bowl until light and fluffy. Add the eggs one at a time, beating well after each addition. Sift the flour, baking powder and nutmeg into a large bowl. Add the remaining cake ingredients and stir to coat the fruit and nuts in the flour mixture. Add to the butter mixture and stir to combine well.

Spoon the mixture into the prepared tin, pushing it into each corner. Bake for 1½–1¾ hours, or until a cake tester inserted into the centre of the cake comes out clean, covering the cake with foil if it browns too quickly. Remove from the oven and leave to cool in the tin for 30 minutes, then turn out onto a wire rack to cool completely.

Meanwhile, make the topping. Put the marmalade in a small heatproof bowl, stir in 2 tablespoons water, then sprinkle the gelatine over the top. Set the bowl over a small saucepan of simmering water, ensuring the base of the bowl doesn't touch the water, and stir until the gelatine has dissolved.

Brush the top of the cooled cake with some of the gelatine mixture and arrange the glacé fruit and almonds over the top. Brush or drizzle with the remaining gelatine mixture and allow to set.

Glacé fruit and nut cake will keep for up to 3 months, wrapped in baking paper and stored in a cool place in an airtight container.

fruit & nut bread

makes 1 loaf

280 g (10 oz/2¼ cups) plain
(all-purpose) flour

2 teaspoons active dried yeast

1 teaspoon mixed (pumpkin pie)
spice

2 tablespoons caster (superfine)
sugar

2 teaspoons grated orange zest

40 g (1½ oz/⅓ cup) sultanas
(golden raisins)

35 g (1¼ oz/¼ cup) currants

1 tablespoon mixed peel (mixed
candied citrus peel)

30 g (1 oz/¼ cup) chopped
pecans

1 egg

80 ml (2½ fl oz/⅓ cup) orange
juice

30 g (1 oz) unsalted butter, melted
oil or melted butter, for brushing

glaze

1 tablespoon milk

1 tablespoon sugar

Sift the flour into a large bowl. Add the yeast, mixed spice, sugar, orange zest, sultanas, currants, mixed peel and pecans and mix well. Make a well in the centre.

In another bowl, mix together the egg, orange juice, butter and 80 ml (2½ fl oz/⅓ cup) warm water, then pour into the well in the fruit mixture. Mix to a soft dough using a wooden spoon.

Turn the dough out onto a lightly floured work surface and knead for 10 minutes, or until smooth and elastic, adding a little extra flour if the dough is sticky. Place the dough in a large oiled bowl, turning to coat in the oil. Cover with plastic wrap and leave to rise in a draught-free place for 45 minutes, or until well risen.

Knock back the dough by punching it gently, then turn out onto a lightly floured work surface and knead for 1 minute. Shape into an oblong or round and place in a greased 20 x 10 cm (8 x 4 inch) loaf (bar) tin, or on a greased baking tray, patting out to a 23 cm (9 inch) circle.

Brush the loaf with oil or melted butter. Cover with a tea towel (dish towel) and leave to rise in a draught-free place for 30 minutes. Meanwhile, preheat the oven to 180°C (350°F/Gas 4).

Bake the bread for 20–30 minutes, or until it is light brown and sounds hollow when tapped on the base. Turn out onto a wire rack to cool. While the bread is still hot, brush with the combined glaze ingredients. Serve warm or cold. Fruit and nut bread is best eaten the day it is made, but can be frozen in an airtight container for up to 6 weeks.

honey & pine nut tart

serves 6-8

250 g (9 oz/2 cups) plain
 (all-purpose) flour
1½ tablespoons icing
 (confectioners') sugar
115 g (4 oz) cold unsalted butter,
 chopped
1 egg, mixed with 2 tablespoons
 iced water

filling
235 g (8½ oz/1½ cups) pine nuts
175 g (6 oz/½ cup) honey
115 g (4 oz) unsalted butter,
 softened
115 g (4 oz/½ cup) caster
 (superfine) sugar
3 eggs
¼ teaspoon natural vanilla
 extract
1 tablespoon almond liqueur
1 teaspoon finely grated lemon
 zest
1 tablespoon lemon juice

icing (confectioners') sugar,
 for dusting
crème fraîche or mascarpone
 cheese, to serve

Lightly grease a fluted, loose-based tart tin measuring 25 cm (10 inches) in diameter and 3.5 cm (1½ inches) deep.

Sift the flour and icing sugar into a large bowl. Using your fingertips, lightly rub in the butter until the mixture resembles fine breadcrumbs. Make a well in the centre, then add the egg to the well. Mix using a flat-bladed knife until a rough dough forms. Turn out onto a lightly floured work surface, then gently press into a ball. Roll out to a circle 3 mm (⅛ inch) thick. Roll the pastry around the rolling pin, then lift and ease it into the prepared tin, gently pressing to fit the side. Trim the edges.

Roll out the pastry scraps and cut out three leaf shapes for decoration. Cover the pastry case and leaves with plastic wrap and refrigerate for 30 minutes. Meanwhile, preheat the oven to 190°C (375°F/Gas 5) and place a baking tray on the middle shelf.

Prick the base of the chilled pastry case with a fork. Line with baking paper and half-fill with baking beads, rice or dried beans. Bake on the heated tray for 10 minutes, then remove the tart, leaving the tray in the oven. Reduce the oven temperature to 180°C (350°F/Gas 4).

To make the filling, spread the pine nuts on a baking tray and roast in the oven for 3–5 minutes, or until golden. Heat the honey in a small saucepan until liquid, then cool.

Using electric beaters, cream the butter and sugar until light and fluffy. Add the eggs one at a time, beating well after each addition. Stir in the pine nuts, remaining filling ingredients and a pinch of salt. Spoon into the tart case, smooth over the surface and arrange three pastry leaves in the centre.

Place the tart tin back on the hot baking tray and bake for 20 minutes, or until the filling is golden. Cover the top with foil and bake for a further 20 minutes, or until the filling has set. Remove from the oven and leave to cool in the tin.

Serve warm or at room temperature, dusted with icing sugar and with a dollop of crème fraîche or mascarpone.

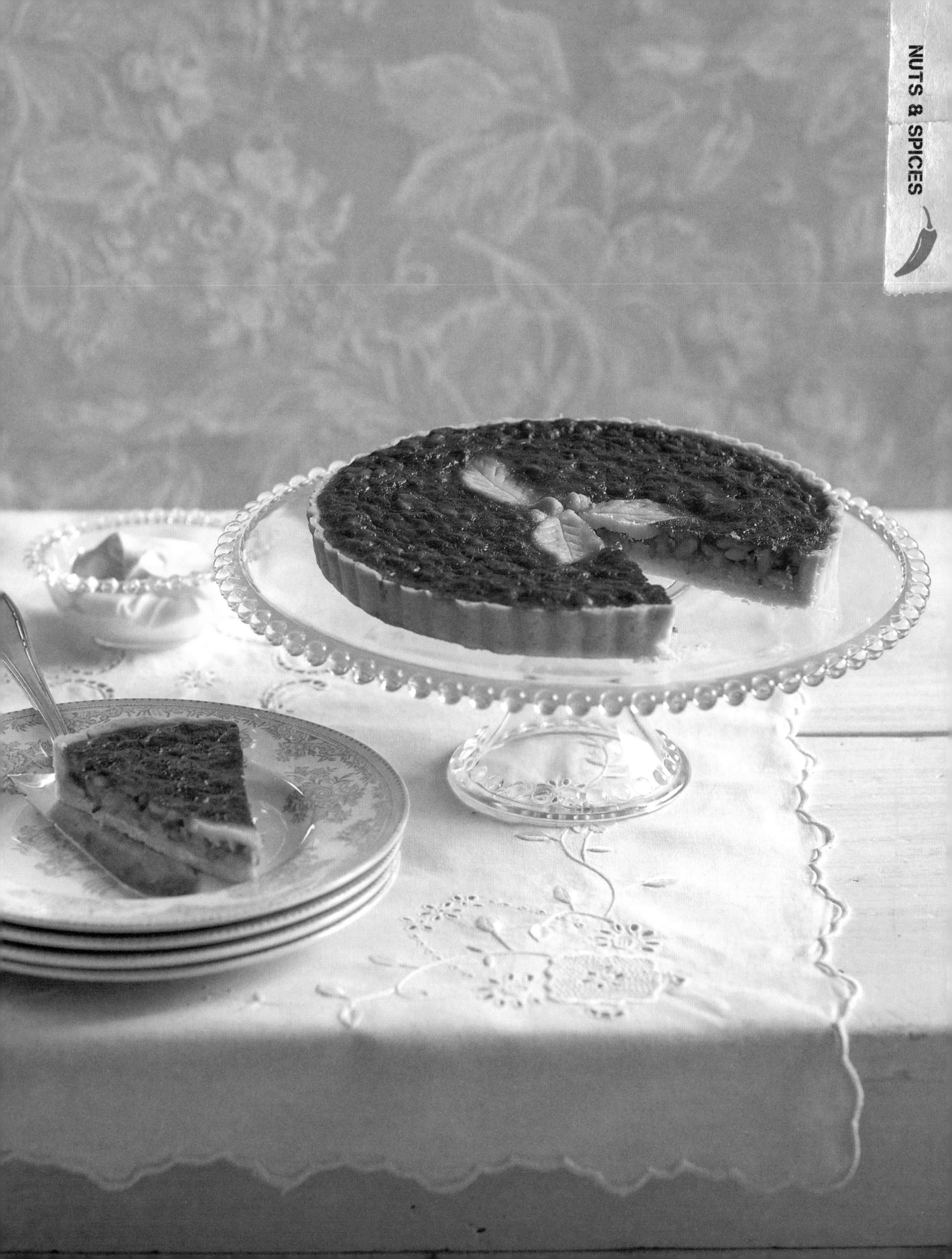

cardamom kulfi

makes 8

2 litres (70 fl oz/8 cups) milk
10 green cardamom pods, lightly crushed
110 g (3¾ oz/½ cup) sugar
2 tablespoons almonds, blanched and finely chopped

3 tablespoons unsalted pistachio nuts, skinned and finely chopped
edible silver leaf (varak) (optional)

Put the milk and cardamom pods in a heavy-based saucepan and bring to the boil. Reduce the heat to low and simmer, stirring frequently, for about 2 hours, or until the milk has reduced to a third of the original amount, about 750 ml (26 fl oz/3 cups). Whenever a thin skin forms on top, stir it back in.

Add the sugar to the pan and stir unitl it dissolves, simmer for 5 minutes, then cool slightly and strain the mixture into a shallow non-metallic dish. Add the almonds and half the pistachios to the dish and put in the freezer. Put 8 x 125 ml (4 fl oz/½ cup) dariole moulds in the freezer to chill.

Every 20 minutes remove the kulfi dish from the freezer and, using electric beaters or a fork, give the kulfi a good whisk to break up the ice crystals. When the mixture is stiff, divide it among the moulds and freeze until hardened completely. Dip the moulds in hot water and turn out the kulfi. Sprinkle with the remaining pistachios and decorate with a piece of edible silver leaf, if using.

vodka & juniper cured salmon

serves 6-8

10 juniper berries

2 tablespoons sea salt

2 large handfuls dill, chopped

grated zest of 1 lime

60 ml (2 fl oz/¼ cup) vodka

3 teaspoons caster (superfine) sugar

500 g (1 lb 2 oz) boneless, skinless salmon fillet

lemon wedges, to serve

mustard and dill sauce

1 tablespoon dijon mustard

1 teaspoon caster (superfine) sugar

100 ml (3½ fl oz) sunflower oil

2 teaspoons white wine vinegar

1 large handful dill, chopped

Roughly crush the juniper berries using a mortar and pestle or spice grinder. In a shallow non-metallic dish, combine the sea salt, 2 teaspoons freshly ground black pepper, the dill, juniper, lime zest, vodka and sugar and spread the mixture evenly in the dish. Lay the salmon in the dish and cover the fish with plastic wrap. Top the salmon with a slightly smaller dish filled with a heavy weight and refrigerate for 48 hours, turning the salmon over every 12 hours.

Mix the mustard and sugar together in a bowl and gradually whisk in the oil until combined. Stir in the vinegar, dill and 1 tablespoon boiling water and season to taste.

Remove the salmon from the marinade. Gently scrape off any excess marinade and pat dry. Using a sharp knife, cut the salmon into thin slices. Drizzle the salmon with the mustard and dill sauce and serve with rye bread and lemon wedges.

mussels in galangal & kaffir leaf broth

serves 4

6 cm (2½ inch) piece of fresh galangal, peeled and sliced

1 lemon grass stem, white part only, finely sliced

1 kg (2 lb 4 oz) mussels, beards removed and scrubbed

310 ml (10¾ fl oz/1¼ cups) coconut milk

2 tablespoons green curry paste

4 kaffir lime leaves, finely shredded

1 teaspoon sugar, plus extra to taste

1 tablespoon fish sauce

1 handful coriander (cilantro) leaves

1 handful mint

Fill a large frying pan with 500 ml (17 fl oz/2 cups) water and bring to the boil. Add the galangal and lemon grass to the frying pan and cook for 2 minutes. Add the mussels, cover tightly and cook for 5 minutes, shaking the pan. Discard any unopened mussels. Remove the mussels from the pan and set aside. Reserve 250 ml (9 fl oz/1 cup) of the stock, the galangal and lemon grass.

In a wok, bring the coconut milk to the boil. Add the curry paste, lime leaves and sugar. Stir and simmer for 3 minutes, or until the oil comes to the surface. Add the reserved galangal and lemon grass and simmer for a further 2 minutes. Add the mussels to the wok and stir until the mussels are covered with the sauce. Add the fish sauce and extra sugar, to taste, and enough of the reserved stock to adjust flavours, and mix well. To serve, divide the mussels among four bowls and top with the fresh herbs.

chilli jam

fills 4 x 250 ml (9 fl oz/1 cup) jars

500 g (1 lb 2 oz) red capsicums
(peppers), cut into large pieces

120 g (4¼ oz) fresh long red
chillies, seeded

310 ml (10¾ fl oz/1¼ cups) white
vinegar

880 g (1 lb 15 oz/4 cups) sugar

185 g (6½ oz/1 cup lightly packed)
soft brown sugar

Cook the capsicum pieces, skin side up, under a hot grill (broiler) until
the skin blackens and blisters. Put in a plastic bag and cool, then remove
the skin. Put the capsicum and chilli in a food processor with 60 ml
(2 fl oz/¼ cup) of the vinegar and process until finely chopped.

Put the capsicum and chilli mixture in a large saucepan and add the
remaining vinegar. Bring to the boil, then reduce the heat and simmer
for 8 minutes. Remove from the heat. Add the sugars and stir until
all the sugar has dissolved, then return to the heat and boil for
5–10 minutes, or until it has thickened slightly.

Spoon immediately into 4 x 250 ml (9 fl oz/1 cup) very clean, warm glass
jars and seal. Turn the jars upside down for 2 minutes, then invert and
leave to cool. Leave for 1 month before opening to allow the flavours to
develop. Store in a cool, dark place for up to 12 months. Refrigerate after
opening for up to 6 weeks.

gingerbread

makes about 40

350 g (12 oz) plain (all-purpose)
  flour

2 teaspoons baking powder

2 teaspoons ground ginger

100 g (3½ oz) chilled unsalted
  butter, diced

175 g (6 oz/¾ cup) soft brown
  sugar

1 egg, beaten

115 g (4 oz/⅓ cup) dark treacle

1 egg white

3 teaspoons lemon juice

155 g (5½ oz/1¼ cups) icing
  (confectioners') sugar

1 egg white

200 g (7 oz) icing (confectioners')
  sugar

Preheat the oven to 190°C (375°F/Gas 5). Lightly grease two baking trays.
Sift the flour, baking powder, ginger and a pinch of salt into a bowl. Rub
in the butter until the mixture resembles fine breadcrumbs, then stir in
the sugar. Make a well in the centre, add the egg and treacle and, using
a wooden spoon, stir until a soft dough forms. Transfer to a clean surface
and knead until smooth.

Divide the dough in half and roll out on a lightly floured work surface
until 5 mm (¼ inch) thick. Using various-shaped cutters, cut into desired
shapes, then transfer to the prepared trays. Bake in batches for
8 minutes, or until the biscuits (cookies) are light-brown. Cool on the
trays for 2–3 minutes, then transfer to a wire rack to cool completely.
(If using the biscuits as hanging decorations, use a skewer to make a
small hole in each one while still hot.)

To make the glaze, whisk the egg white and lemon juice together until
foamy, then whisk in the icing sugar to form a smooth, thin icing. Cover
the surface with plastic wrap until needed. To make the royal icing,
lightly whisk the egg white until just foamy, then gradually whisk in
enough icing sugar to form a soft icing. Cover the surface with plastic
wrap until needed. Brush a thin layer of glaze over some of the biscuits
and leave to set. Using an icing bag (see Note) filled with royal icing,
decorate the biscuits as desired. Store glazed gingerbread for up to 3 days
in an airtight container. Un-iced biscuits will keep for up to 2 weeks in
an airtight container.

*Note: To make a paper icing bag, cut a piece of baking paper into a 19
cm (7½ inch) square and then cut in half diagonally to form two triangles.
Hold the triangle, with the longest side away from you, and curl the left
hand point over and in towards the centre. Repeat with the right hand
point, forming a cone shape, with both ends meeting neatly in the middle.
Staple together at the wide end.*

poached pears in saffron syrup

serves 4

1 vanilla bean, split lengthways
½ teaspoon saffron threads
185 g (6½ oz) caster (superfine)
  sugar

2 teaspoons grated lemon zest
4 pears, peeled

Put the vanilla bean, saffron threads, sugar, lemon zest and 500 ml (17 fl oz/2 cups) water in a large saucepan and mix together well. Stir over low heat until the sugar has dissolved. Bring to the boil over high heat, then reduce to a gentle simmer. Add the pears and cook, covered, for 12–15 minutes, or until tender when tested with a metal skewer. Turn the pears over with a slotted spoon halfway through cooking. Once cooked, remove from the syrup with a slotted spoon, set aside and cover to keep warm.

Allow the saffron syrup to come to the boil and cook uncovered for 8–10 minutes, or until the syrup has reduced by half and thickened slightly. Serve the pears with the sauce spooned over and some whipped cream on the side.

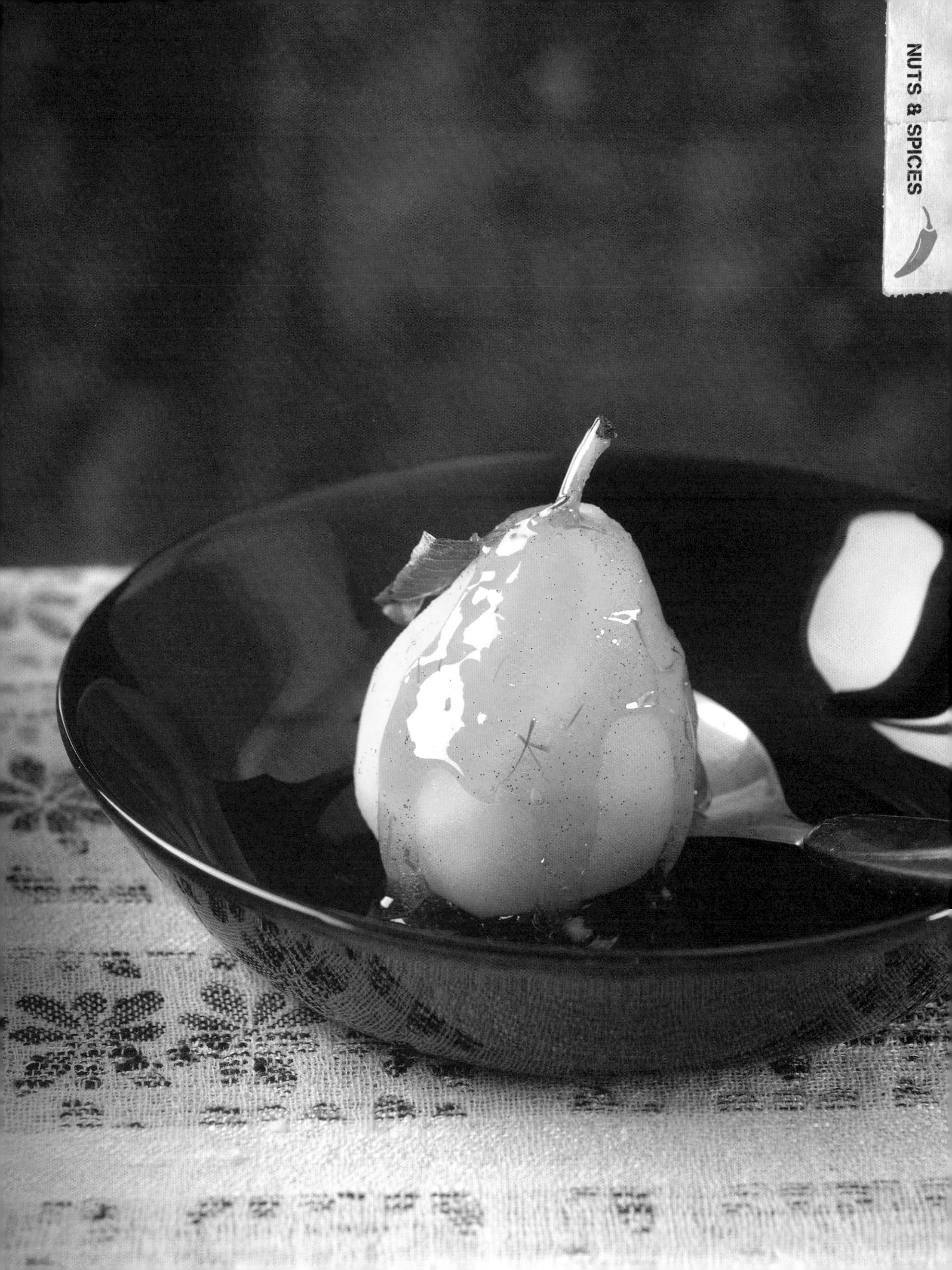

turmeric, ginger & lime chicken skewers

serves 4

8 boneless, skinless chicken thighs
4 limes

marinade
250 ml (9 fl oz/1 cup) coconut
    milk
2 teaspoons ground turmeric
2 tablespoons finely grated
fresh ginger

1 tablespoon finely chopped lemon
    grass, white part only
2 garlic cloves, crushed
juice of 1 lime
1 tablespoon fish sauce
2 teaspoons grated palm sugar
    (jaggery)

Cut the chicken into 3 cm (1¼ inch) squares. Mix all the marinade ingredients in a non-metallic bowl and add the chicken pieces. Cover and refrigerate for 2 hours.

Soak 8 bamboo skewers in cold water for 20 minutes. Thread the chicken onto the skewers. Cut the limes in half crossways.

Preheat a barbecue hotplate to medium–high heat. Cook the skewers on the hotplate for 5 minutes, then turn and cook for a further 5 minutes, or until cooked through. Cook the limes, cut side down, on the hotplate over medium–high heat for 4–5 minutes, or until caramelized. Serve the skewers with rice, along with the limes for squeezing over the chicken.

chocolate star anise cake with coffee caramel cream

serves 8

200 g (7 oz) good-quality dark
    chocolate, roughly chopped

125 g (4½ oz) unsalted butter

4 eggs

2 egg yolks

115 g (4 oz/½ cup) caster
    (superfine) sugar

50 g (1¾ oz) plain (all-purpose)
    flour, sifted

2 teaspoons ground star anise

55 g (2 oz/½ cup) ground
    almonds

coffee caramel cream

125 ml (4 fl oz/½ cup) thick
    (double/heavy) cream

45 g (1½ oz/¼ cup) soft brown
    sugar

2 tablespoons brewed espresso
    coffee, cooled

Preheat the oven to 190°C (375°F/Gas 5). Grease and line a 23 cm (9 inch) spring-form cake tin. Put the chocolate and butter in a bowl set over a saucepan of gently simmering water, but do not allow the base of the bowl to come into contact with the water. Heat gently until the mixture is melted.

Put the eggs, egg yolks and sugar into a bowl and beat with electric beaters for 5 minutes, or until thickened. Fold in the flour, ground star anise and ground almonds and then fold in the melted chocolate mixture until evenly combined (the mixture should be runny at this stage). Pour the mixture into the prepared tin and bake for 30–35 minutes, or until a skewer inserted in the middle comes out clean. Cool in the tin for 5 minutes and then remove and cool on a wire rack.

To make the coffee caramel cream, whip the cream, sugar and coffee together until soft peaks form and the colour is a pale caramel. Serve the cold cake cut into wedges with a spoonful of the coffee caramel cream.

patatas bravas

serves 6

1 kg (2 lb 4 oz) all-purpose
  potatoes, such as desiree
oil, for deep-frying
500 g (1 lb 2 oz) ripe roma (plum)
  tomatoes
2 tablespoons olive oil
¼ red onion, finely chopped

2 garlic cloves, crushed
3 teaspoons sweet Spanish paprika
¼ teaspoon cayenne pepper
1 bay leaf
1 teaspoon caster (superfine) sugar
1 handful flat-leaf (Italian) parsley,
  chopped, to garnish

Peel, then cut the potatoes into 2 cm (¾ inch) cubes. Rinse, then drain well and pat completely dry. Fill a deep-fryer or large, heavy-based saucepan one-third full of oil and heat to 180°C (350°F), or until a cube of bread dropped in the oil browns in 15 seconds. Cook the potato in batches for 5 minutes, or until golden. Drain well on paper towel and cool completely. Do not discard the oil.

Score a cross in the base of each tomato. Put in a bowl of boiling water for 10 seconds, then plunge into cold water and peel the skin away from the cross. Chop the flesh.

Heat the olive oil in a saucepan over medium heat and cook the onion for 3 minutes, or until softened. Add the garlic, paprika and cayenne pepper and cook for 1–2 minutes, or until fragrant.

Add the tomato, bay leaf, sugar and 90 ml (3 fl oz) water and cook, stirring occasionally, for 20 minutes, or until thick and pulpy. Cool slightly and remove the bay leaf. Blend in a food processor until smooth, adding a little water if necessary. Before serving, return the sauce to the saucepan and simmer over low heat for 2 minutes, or until heated through. Season well.

Reheat the oil to 180°C (350°F) and cook the potato again, in batches, for 2 minutes, or until very crisp and golden. Drain on paper towel. This second frying makes the potato extra crispy and stops the sauce soaking in immediately.

Spoon the sauce over the potatoes. Garnish with the parsley and serve.

eggplant, tahini & mint salad

Serves 4

tahini dressing
65 g (2¼ oz/¼ cup) tahini
2 teaspoons olive oil
1 garlic clove, crushed
2 tablespoons lemon juice

1 large eggplant (aubergine), thinly
   sliced
2 tablespoons olive oil

1 garlic clove, crushed
1 large handful mint, roughly
   chopped
2 handfuls flat-leaf (Italian)
   parsley, chopped
2 tablespoons thick, creamy, plain
   yoghurt
¼ teaspoon mild smoked Spanish
   paprika

Put all the tahini dressing ingredients in a food processor with 125 ml
(4 fl oz/½ cup) warm water. Blend until well combined and set aside
until needed.

Preheat a barbecue grill plate, hotplate or chargrill pan to medium. Put
the eggplant slices in a large bowl, add the oil and garlic, then toss well
to coat. Cook the eggplant on one side for about 1½ minutes, or until
grill marks appear, turn over and cook for a further 1½ minutes. Put in
a large bowl and allow to cool.

Toss the mint, parsley and tahini dressing through the eggplant slices,
mixing well. Serve at room temperature, dolloped with yoghurt and
sprinkled with the paprika.

hazelnut & blueberry shortcake

Serves 8

100 g (3½ oz/ ¾ cup) whole hazelnuts

280 g (10 oz/ 2¼ cups) self-raising flour

1½ teaspoons ground cinnamon

165 g (5¾ oz/ ¾ cup) raw (demerara) sugar, plus extra, for sprinkling

150 g (5½ oz) unsalted butter, chopped

2 eggs

160 g (5¾ oz/ ½ cup) blueberry jam

fresh blueberries, to serve

whipped or thick (double/heavy) cream, to serve

Grease a 20 cm (8 inch) round, deep cake tin and line the base with baking paper.

Spread the whole hazelnuts on a baking tray and bake for 5–10 minutes, or until lightly golden. Place in a clean tea towel (dish towel) and rub together to remove the skins, then roughly chop the nuts.

Put the flour, cinnamon, sugar, butter and half the hazelnuts in a food processor and blend until the nuts are finely chopped. Add eggs and blend until just combined. Press half the mixture onto the base of the prepared tin, then spread the blueberry jam evenly over the top.

Lightly knead the remaining hazelnuts into the remaining cake dough, then press evenly over the jam layer. Sprinkle with extra sugar and bake for 50 minutes, or until a cake tester inserted in the centre of the cake comes out clean. Remove from oven and leave to cool in the tin for 15 minutes, before turning out onto a wire rack to cool completely.

Cut into wedges and serve with fresh blueberries and cream.

Blueberry and hazelnut shortcake will keep for 2–3 days, stored in a cool place in an airtight container, or can be frozen in an airtight container for up to 6 weeks.

SELECTION & STORAGE

The art of selecting and storing spices

With a few handy hints you can keep your spices fresh and fragrant – and wow your dinner guests.

The sweet aroma of freshly ground cinnamon, the warmth of roasted cumin and the spicy fragrance of grated nutmeg are enough to convince any keen cook of the importance of maintaining a good spice pantry. The most important thing is to buy small quantities of whole spices and grind them only as you need them. The volatile oils, responsible for giving spices their kick, fade over time, taking with them the spice's true flavour, colour and aroma.

SPICE TIPS

Be harsh

If the spices in your pantry are past their use-by date, throw them out. Replacing them is a small price to pay for the difference between a great curry and an average one. To test for freshness, give them a quick sniff or, for spices that naturally yield little aroma, rub them lightly between your fingers to release the volatile oils. If there is a discernible aroma, they should be fine, otherwise it simply isn't worth it—no matter how much of the spice you may add.

Pick the package

Avoid buying spices packaged in cardboard or cellophane, since the volatile oils become oxygenated and deteriorate rapidly. 'High barrier materials' such as glass jars with airtight metal lids are the ideal storage solution and should be stored away from light and heat. While the exotic appeal of large open sacks of spices in Moroccan souks is often irresistible, unless there is an extremely high turnover, the spices will have suffered the ravages of heat, light and humidity. Likewise, spice racks provide a wonderful visual, but are better placed on the back of a cupboard door or somewhere away from direct sunlight.

Buy whole spices

The aroma of freshly roasted and ground spices is incomparable. Where possible, buy whole spices in small quantities and grind them only as you need them. Many spices benefit from a light dry roasting before use, since it helps release the volatile oils. Place the spices in a dry frying pan and shake over low heat until they start to release their aroma. Remove from the heat, allow to cool, then grind. Take care not to burn the spices or they will become bitter.

Have the right equipment

A small mortar and pestle, spice grinder, or even a small electric coffee grinder is essential. A large mortar and pestle is handy if you want to make your own curry, chilli or herb pastes such as harissa and chermoula, although these can also be made quite successfully in a food processor. To remove the lingering aromas from your spice blender, follow up by grinding cane sugar or rice.

Buy the best quality

It is worth seeking out a spice vendor with a high turnover and who pays attention to quality and packaging. You will sometimes find seed spices still have extraneous husks and stems mixed through them, which can end up compromising the appearance and texture of many dishes. Good spice vendors will only sell those that have been sieved of all else but the seed.

baharat spice mix
makes 2 tablespoons

2 teaspoons black
   peppercorns

2 teaspoons
   coriander seeds

2 teaspoons cumin
   seeds

2 teaspoons cloves

seeds from 6 green
   cardamom pods

½ cinnamon stick,
   broken into small
   pieces

1 teaspoon Hungarian
   paprika

1 teaspoon ground
   nutmeg

Dry-fry all the spices, except the paprika and nutmeg,
in a frying pan over medium heat until fragrant. Cool,
then put in a food processor or spice mill with the
paprika and nutmeg. Blend until finely ground. Store in
an airtight container for up to 1 month.

cajun spice mix
makes 4 tablespoons

1 tablespoon garlic
   powder

1 tablespoon onion
   powder

2 teaspoons white
   pepper

2 teaspoons freshly
   ground black pepper

1½ teaspoons cayenne
   pepper

2 teaspoons dried
   thyme

½ teaspoon dried
   oregano

Mix all the ingredients in a small bowl until well combined.
Store in an airtight container for up
to 1 month.

berbere spice mix
makes 3 tablespoons

1 tablespoon cumin
   seeds

1 tablespoon coriander
   seeds

½ teaspoon allspice
   berries

½ teaspoon ajowan

1 teaspoon black
   peppercorns

½ teaspoon fenugreek

1 teaspoon chilli flakes

¼ teaspoon cloves

½ teaspoon sea salt

Dry-fry the cumin seeds, coriander seeds and allspice
berries separately in a dry frying pan over high heat for
30 seconds, or until fragrant. Transfer to a mortar, then
add remaining ingredients and pound with a pestle until
coarsely ground. Store in an airtight container for up to
1 month.

SELECTION & STORAGE

chaat masala
makes 10 tablespoons

2 teaspoons
  fennel seeds

seeds from 2 green
  cardamom pods

2 tablespoons
  coriander seeds

2 tablespoons
  cumin seeds

1 teaspoon
  ajowan

3 tablespoons black
  salt

1 tablespoon
  amchoor powder

2 dried red chillies

1 teaspoon black
  peppercorns

1 teaspoon
  pomegranate
  seeds

Dry-fry the fennel, cardamom, coriander, cumin and ajowan in a dry frying pan over high heat for 30 seconds, or until fragrant. Grind the roasted mixture to a fine powder with the other ingredients, using a spice grinder or mortar and pestle. Store in an airtight container for up to 1 month.

dukkah
makes 250 ml (9 fl oz/1 cup)

50 g (1¾ oz/⅓ cup)
  white sesame seeds

2 tablespoons
  coriander seeds

1 tablespoon cumin
  seeds

50 g (1¾ oz/⅓ cup)
  hazelnuts, chopped

1 teaspoon salt

½ teaspoon freshly
  ground black pepper

Heat a frying pan and separately dry-fry the sesame, coriander and cumin seeds and the hazelnuts for 1–2 minutes, or until they brown and start to release their aroma. Allow to cool and then process to a coarse powder in a food processor or mortar and pestle. Transfer to a bowl and season with the salt and pepper.

garam masala
makes 4 tablespoons

10 green cardamom
  pods

1 cinnamon stick

2 tablespoons cumin
  seeds

2 teaspoons cloves

1 teaspoon black
  peppercorns

1 teaspoon freshly
  grated nutmeg

Remove the seeds from the cardamom and discard the pods. Break the cinnamon stick into small pieces. Put the cardamom seeds, cinnamon pieces, cumin seeds, whole cloves and black peppercorns in a small frying pan. Dry-fry for 1–2 minutes, or until fragrant. Set aside and cool. Put in a food processor or spice mill with the nutmeg and blend until finely ground. Store in an airtight container for up to 1 month.

mixed (pumpkin pie) spice
makes 2 tablespoons

1 tablespoon ground
  cinnamon

1 teaspoon ground
  coriander

1 teaspoon ground
  nutmeg

½ teaspoon ground
  ginger

¼ teaspoon ground
  allspice

¼ teaspoon ground
  cloves

Put all the spices in a small bowl and combine well. Store in an airtight container for up to 1 month.

pickling spice
makes 4 tablespoons

12 dried small red
  chillies

1 teaspoon yellow
  mustard seeds

1 teaspoon fennel
  seeds

1 teaspoon dill seeds

1 teaspoon allspice

1 teaspoon cloves

1 teaspoon juniper
  berries

4 dried bay leaves,
  crushed

1 cinnamon stick,
  broken into small
  pieces

Put all the spices in a small bowl and combine well. Store in an airtight container for up to 1 month.

panch phora
makes 5 tablespoons

1 tablespoon brown
  mustard seeds

1 tablespoon nigella
  seeds

1 tablespoon cumin
  seeds

1 tablespoon fennel
  seeds

1 tablespoon fenugreek
  seeds

Put all the spices in a small bowl and combine well. Store in an airtight container for up to 1 year.

Index

Index

Index

Published in 2012 by Murdoch Books Pty Limited

Murdoch Books Australia
Pier 8/9
23 Hickson Road
Millers Point NSW 2000
Phone: +61 (0) 2 8220 2000
Fax: +61 (0) 2 8220 2558
www.murdochbooks.com.au
info@murdochbooks.com.au

Murdoch Books UK Limited
Erico House, 6th Floor
93–99 Upper Richmond Road
Putney, London SW15 2TG
Phone: +44 (0) 20 8785 5995
Fax: +44 (0) 20 8785 5985
www.murdochbooks.co.uk
info@murdochbooks.co.uk

For Corporate Orders & Custom Publishing contact Noel Hammond,
National Business Development Manager Murdoch Books Australia

Chief Executive: Matt Handbury
Publishing Director: Chris Rennie

Designer: Clare O'Loughlin
Project Manager: Liz Malcolm
Editor: Gabriella Sterio
Editorial Coordinator: Martina Vascotto
Indexer: Jo Rudd
Production: Joan Beal

National Library of Australia Cataloguing-in-Publication Data
The farmer's market family cookbook
ISBN: 9781742663401 (pbk.)
Includes index.
Cooking.
641.5

A catalogue record for this book is available from the British Library.

Printed by 1010 Printing International Limited, China